Outside the London Hippodrome, 1922

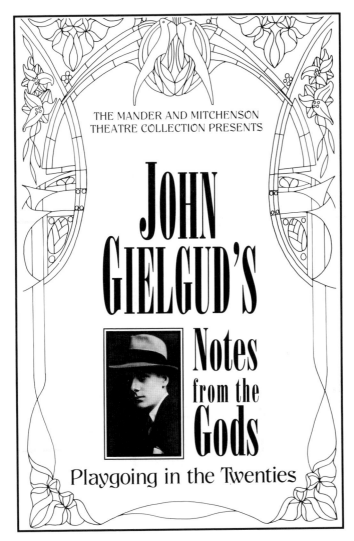

THE MANDER AND MITCHENSON
THEATRE COLLECTION PRESENTS

JOHN GIELGUD'S

Notes from the Gods

Playgoing in the Twenties

edited by Richard Mangan

NICK HERN BOOKS • LONDON

A NICK HERN BOOK

John Gielgud's Notes from the Gods
first published in Great Britain in 1994
by Nick Hern Books,
14 Larden Road, London W3 7ST

Designed and typeset by
Ned Hoste, 2H,
94a Lordship Lane,
London SE22 8HF

Printed and bound in Great Britain by
Biddles Ltd, Guildford and King's Lynn

British Cataloguing in Publication Data
A catalogue record for this book is available
from the British Library

ISBN 1-85459 105 3

PREFACE

Raymond Mander and Joe Mitchenson started what was to become one of the world's finest collections of theatrical memorabilia in the late 1930s. Like most people who worked in the theatre, I was aware of the Collection's riches and had had occasion to turn to them for their advice and expertise several times.

I became Director of the Collection in 1988 when Joe Mitchenson was still alive and working, Raymond Mander having died in 1983. To acquire an awareness and working knowledge of the Collection was (and still is) a major undertaking, but Joe's encyclopaedic memory was of incalculable value in the process. I therefore set about going through the one thousand or so archive boxes in a naively optimistic effort to do so! It was whilst doing this that my eye one day happened to light upon a programme with tiny but eminently legible handwriting on the cover. Having worked with him several times in the past, I immediately recognised it as that of Sir John Gielgud. In response to my query, Joe told me that sometime in the 1950s, Sir John's mother had given the Collection many such programmes, together with letters and cuttings relating to his career.

Eventually I managed to discover around three hundred programmes from Sir John's early theatregoing days between 1917 (when he was 13) and 1925. I was fascinated and struck by the breadth of his visits, the increasingly perceptible acuity of his vision of what he saw, the strength of his opinions and the skill with which he expressed them. Even at this early age, one was aware that here was indeed a true 'homme de théâtre', with an interest in every aspect of the subject – acting, directing, design, music and writing.

Nick Hern shared my enthusiasm for my findings. Sir John was approached for his permission and, with his customary generosity, gave the project his blessing. When we had made our selection, we sent it to him for his comments and, we hoped, his approval. Not only did we get the latter, but a great number of annotations from that prodigious memory going back some 75 years, and these have been added as footnotes to the text marked J.G., 1993.

The Trustees of the Collection and I are indebted to Sir John not only for his support given to Raymond and Joe over many years, but also for his great kindness and help with this book, the proceeds of which will be of great assistance in ensuring the survival of the Collection.

It is therefore dedicated with great affection to Sir John and to Raymond Mander and Joe Mitchenson, without whom...

RICHARD MANGAN

INTRODUCTION

The fifteen year old John Gielgud was still a day boy at Westminster School at the beginning of 1920. His decision to become an actor would be made during this year, and although his parents were not enthusiastic, he persuaded them to let him try; if he did not succeed before he was twenty-five, he would bow to their wishes and become an architect. As a member of the famous Terry family, his links with the world of the theatre were already strong, and, with his brothers Lewis and Val and his sister Eleanor, he was taken by his parents and friends to many shows.

We first encounter him at 'Mary Rose', which he clearly saw on an unaccompanied visit...

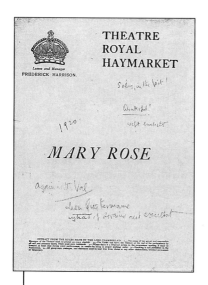

'**Solus, in the pit!**

Wonderful! wept buckets.

Later visit.

Again with Val.

Leon Quartermaine instead of Loraine and excellent.'

Perhaps the first recorded account of the famous Gielgud tear ducts in action - he was sixteen. This was the first production of Barrie's most enigmatic play, based on the idea that all ghosts are really women looking for their lost children - echoes of Peter Pan. The play was an early success for the young Fay Compton, who later in her long and distinguished career played Ophelia to John Barrymore's Hamlet in 1925 and to Gielgud's Hamlet in 1939. Her leading man in the picture, Leon Quartermaine, was an actor with whom Gielgud worked many times and admired greatly: he became the third of Fay Compton's four husbands.

'*Arthur Whitby and Mary Jerrold, both superb Barrie actors, were excellent as the parents of Mary Rose, Jean Cadell perfect as the housekeeper, but Ernest Thesiger, a brilliant eccentric, was quite unconvincing as a Scotch gillie, though he boasted at this time that he had been coached by an authentic member of the clan who would take him for walks in the Park to try out his accent.*

'*The island that liked to be visited' in which the second act took place was very lacking in atmosphere - I thought it should be mistily romantic with silver birches.*'

J.G.,1993

Fay Compton as Mary Rose, Leon Quartermaine as Simon Blake

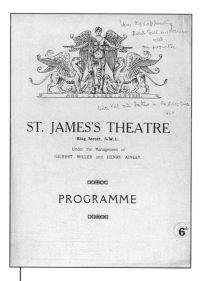

ST. JAMES'S THEATRE

King Street, S.W.1.

Under the Management of
GILBERT MILLER and HENRY AINLEY.

ᗌᗌᗋᗋ

PROGRAMME

ᗌᗌᗋᗋ

6ᵈ·

'With Val and Father in the Dress Circle.

Very disappointing. Basil Gill and Rosmer good. Nice production.'

Claude Rains, who played Casca and was also the Stage Manager, would later be one of Gielgud's teachers at the Academy of Dramatic Art. In later years, Gielgud was questioned about Rains by an American television interviewer; dropping one of his famous 'bricks', he replied 'I think he failed and went to America.'

Henry Ainley was one of the leading romantic juveniles of the day, extremely handsome and possessed of a beautiful voice. Illness in his late forties prevented him from reaching the heights of his profession.

Gielgud himself would later play Mark Antony at the Old Vic in 1930, Cassius at Stratford in 1950 and on film in 1952, and Julius Caesar at the National Theatre in 1977.

Val (Gielgud), John's elder brother worked briefly in the theatre before becoming a distinguished radio producer and playwright, and Head of BBC Drama.

'Actually I was devoted to Claude Rains, and tried to model my early performances on many of his that I saw from the front - notably at the Everyman, Hampstead, his Dubedat in 'The Doctor's Dilemma' and as Napoleon in 'The Man of Destiny'. He appeared with Ainley in a play 'The Jest' in which Lionel and John Barrymore had had a huge success in America. But Rains got all the notices on the pre-London tour and Ainley decided not to bring it in. (It was later produced as 'The Love Thief' with Norman McKinnel, Cathleen Nesbitt and Ernest Thesiger and was a complete failure.) When I asked Rains why he was going to America he answered sadly "My dear chap, I can't eat my notices."'

J.G.,1993

4

Milton Rosmer (L) as Cassius, probably Henry Morrell (R) as Pindarus

Henry Ainley as
Marcus Antonius

Claude Rains (L) as Casca, Basil Gill (second left) as Marcus Brutus,
Henry Oscar (fifth left) as Metellus Cimber, Milton Rosmer (R) as
Cassius, Henry Ainley (fifth right) as Marcus Antonius

Henry Ainley as Marcus Antonius

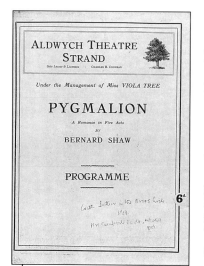

ALDWYCH THEATRE
STRAND
Sole Lessee & Licensee · Charles B. Cochran

Under the Management of Miss VIOLA TREE

PYGMALION

A Romance in Five Acts
BY
BERNARD SHAW

PROGRAMME

With father in the Dress Circle
1914
Mrs Campbell too old, still good
6ᵈ·

'With Father in the Dress Circle.

Mrs Campbell too old, but still good.'

Mrs Patrick Campbell was the first British Eliza in 1914, when she was already 49 years old. This was the first London revival of the play: it ran for 78 performances. Marion Terry, another of Gielgud's great-aunts, played Mrs Higgins.

'Mrs C. had behaved in her usual unpredictable fashion, walking off the stage at a rehearsal when Shaw came in to the stalls and playing the piano in her dressing room.

Marion Terry and she were old rivals from the St James's Theatre days with Alexander, but presumably agreed to bury the hatchet on this occasion. Aubrey Smith, a tactful and valuable member of any company, must have provided a much needed measure of patience and persuasion.

Agnes Thomas was exceedingly good as the housekeeper and Faith Celli, who had made an enormous personal success in Barrie's 'Dear Brutus', played Miss Eynsford-Hill. Mrs Campbell remarked "Who is that girl who sits with her legs akimbo?"'

J.G.,1993

Mrs Patrick Campbell
as Eliza Doolittle

Pictures from the 1914 production at His Majesty's Theatre

'With the Dennyses; also with Katherine and Mother and alone.

Excellent!!!'

Nigel Playfair took over the management of the Lyric Theatre, Hammersmith, in 1918 with financial backing from the novelist Arnold Bennett. He presented his celebrated revival of 'The Beggar's Opera' on 5 June 1920, with the music rearranged by Frederick Austin and decor by Claude Lovat Fraser. It ran for one thousand four hundred and sixty-three performances over three and a half years and was revived several times.

'Playfair has described how Fraser's designs were too expensive and elaborate, and the artist desperately contrived the simple and perfect permanent set, toiling all through the night to finish it. Gordon Craig, who was visiting England at the time, designed and placed the chandelier which hung in one corner of the stage. He also attended a number of performances. The brightly coloured costumes were shorn of trimmings and elaboration, and the elegant stylishness of the whole production, as well as the acting and singing, created a furore. Almost every one of the short songs would be encored, and there were a number of replacements at various times during the incredibly long run. Most of the cast were hitherto unknown, except for the splendid Frederick Ranalow, who graduated from Beecham's opera company to play Macheath. I remember being so familiar with every detail of the production that I resented it when Mrs Peachum's black velvet costume was later replaced by a taffeta one.

So great was my admiration for Playfair's work that I rashly attempted to stage the piece myself at the beginning of the War in 1941, for John Christie's Glyndebourne Company, with his wife Audrey Mildmay as Polly and Michael Redgrave as Macheath. But I persuaded the Motley designers to put the opera into Victorian costumes and settings, and afterwards regretted this decision. It was a dangerous attempt at originality which did not compare with Playfair's.'

J.G.,1993

Violet Marquesita (L) as Lucy Lockit
Frederick Ranalow (C) as Macheath
Sylvia Nelis (R) as Polly Peachum

EVERY EVENING
At 8.15 o'clock

THE BEGGAR'S OPERA
By MR. GAY

New Settings of the Airs and Additional Music by
FREDERIC AUSTIN

CAST

PEACHUM....................FREDERIC AUSTIN
LOCKIT.....................TRISTAN RAWSON
MACHEATH...................FREDERICK RANALOW
FILCH......................SCOTT RUSSELL
THE BEGGAR.................ARNOLD PILBEAM
MRS. PEACHUM...............ELSIE FRENCH
POLLY PEACHUM..............KATHERINE ARKANDY
LUCY LOCKIT................VIOLET MARQUESITA
DIANA TRAPES...............BERYL FREEMAN
JENNY DIVER................ANGELA BADDELEY

Drawer : DAVID HODGES   *Turnkey :* JACK GOSLING

Members of Macheath's Gang :
ALAN TROTTER, MALCOLM RIDDICK, JOHN CLIFFORD,
EDWARD BARRI, CHARLES STEATE

Women of the Town :
ETHEL MAUDE, ELLA MILNE, WINIFRED CHRISTIE,
MILDRED WATSON, ALICE MASON

Period 1728

ACT I. -   PEACHUM'S HOUSE
ACT II. Sc. i. A TAVERN. Near Newgate
          Sc. ii. NEWGATE
ACT III. Sc. i. A STREET
           Sc. ii. NEWGATE
           Sc. iii. THE CONDEMN'D HOLD

Produced by NIGEL PLAYFAIR

Frederick Ranalow as
Macheath, Angela Baddeley
as Jenny Diver

Macheath at the scaffold

*Above: Lockit (Tristan Rawson, L) and Peachum (Scott Russell, R)
take their daughters home*

*Below: Mrs Trapes (Beryl Freeman)
arranging the betrayal of Macheath*

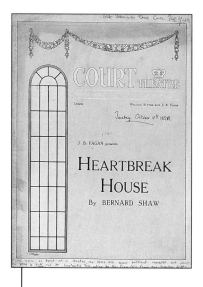

'With Father in the Dress Circle. First Night.

I was never so bored at a theatre, tho' there are some brilliant remarks and ideas. The play is dull, and ill constructed. Good acting by Miss Grey, Miss Evans and Brember Wills.'

The first night of the first English production. Gielgud played very little Shaw throughout his long career; perhaps this early experience is part of the reason why. St John Ervine, the critic of The Observer, also complained about the slowness of the play but attributed this to Shaw's production. He also said, 'People who complain that it is a boring piece would complain of the Book of Job because it is not quite so chirpy as this week's "London Opinion". We need not pay heed to such complainants, but we are entitled to remonstrate with Mr Shaw for playing into their hands.' (The Observer, 23 October 1921)

Mary Grey was a leading actress of the period and was married to the director, J.B. Fagan, whose company Gielgud would later join at the Oxford Playhouse. Gielgud was a great admirer of Edith Evans and would work with her many times in years to come, most memorably perhaps when she played Lady Bracknell in his production of 'The Importance of Being Earnest'.

By October 1921, the seventeen year old John Gielgud was enrolled at the drama school off the Cromwell Road run by Lady Benson, wife of Sir Frank Benson. (It was she who said 'Good Heavens! You walk exactly like a cat with rickets!')

At this time, theatrical students were allowed to work as unpaid supers in crowd scenes at the Old Vic: on 7 November 1921, Gielgud made his first appearance on that stage in a walk-on part in 'Henry V', speaking only one line: 'Here are the numbers of the slaughtered French'.

H.O. Nicholson as Mazzini Dunn
Mary Grey as Hesione Hushabye

'Alone. In the Gallery. First night.

Far too long and under rehearsed. Disappointing scenery. Marvellous clothes. Some good dancing and some dull. Wants pulling together. Very enjoyable otherwise.'

Gielgud's father had been the first to introduce him to the delights of Diaghileff's Russian Ballet, where he was 'enchanted by the brilliant decors and passionate dancing'. (John Gielgud, 'Early Stages'.) At Westminster School one of his best friends was Arnold Haskell, already a confirmed balletomane and later to become a distinguished writer on the ballet. The two of them queued for hours and made several visits to this production for which Bakst designed the decor.

The embryonic director in Gielgud obviously thought more work was needed, and comments on subsequent visits show that this seems to have been done. On a later visit, this time in the stalls, he comments, 'The scenery far better from the floor. The spectacle remains beautiful.'

'Various disasters occurred on this first night. The magic wood refused to grow. The scenery began to emerge from the floor, there was sinister creaking and heaving as it refused to continue upwards, and Lydia Lopokova, The Lilac Fairy, was left pirouetting to and fro waving her wand distractingly as the curtain prematurely fell, while in the final act, the Wedding, she toppled over during a pas de deux and ended sitting on the floor.'

J.G.,1993

Lydia Lopokova as The Lilac Fairy

'Took Billie Bell.
In the Upper Circle.

The best revue I've seen for a long time. Beautifully put on, and a great deal of clever writing, acting and dancing.'

Revues, and in particular C.B. Cochran's spectaculars, were very much the flavour of the time. Gielgud saw most of them, although not all were as well regarded as this.

In spite of his musical talents and sense of humour, the nearest Gielgud ever came to playing in revue was his wartime appearance in some of Noel Coward's playlets from 'Tonight at 8.30'.

'But I have amusing memories of doing a soft shoe shuffle with Carol Channing and Sir Ralph Richardson and a few dance steps with Elton John in a chinky pantomime of Mother Goose.'

J.G.,1993

Juliette Compton

LONDON PAVILION

Proprietors . . . . LONDON PAVILION LTD.

"CHARLES B. COCHRAN'S

FUN OF THE FAYRE"

Revue by JOHN HASTINGS TURNER. Music and Lyrics by AUGUSTUS BARRATT. Additional
Scenes by LAURI WYLIE.
Staged by FRANK COLLINS.
Dances and Ensembles by JACK HASKELL and ROBERT QUINAULT.

PART I.

SCENE 1—Bartholomew Fair, Circa 1685 (Marc Henri and Laverdet)
Costumes designed by LAVERDET and executed by C. ALIAS, Ltd.)
Samuel Pepys	MORRIS HARVEY
Mistress Pepys	MARIE WRIGHT
Lady Castlemaine	IRENE BROWNE
A Citizen	DRELINCOURT ODLUM
His Wife	MELVIA STEWART
Nell Gwynne	EVELYN LAYE
Charles II.	HENRY CAINE
Rope Walker	REGINA FRATELLINI
2 Tumblers	PAOLA FRATELLINI FRANCOIS FRATELLINI
A Monkey	VICTOR FRATELLINI
A Trainer	ALBERT FRATELLINI
2 Countrymen	PARISH & PERU.

Citizens, etc.: BABS MAY, MARY DAVIS, LALLA COLLINS, GRACE KENWICK,
BARBARA MILLS, CONSTANCE HUNTINGTON, LAINE MAY, NELLIE CLIFT, IDA RUSSELL,
DOROTHY NEWTON, IDA PARKINSON, PAMELA DAVIES, MARJORIE SEXTON.

Tumblers, Booth Proprietors,
Clowns, Courtiers, etc.: JO MONSENDER, ARTHUR THACKER, HARRY DANBY, WILFRED
NORMAN, DONALD HANNAY, JOHN HALE, ALAN PIGGOTT, JOSEPH LAURILLARD.

Musical Number:
" I don't want to be a Lady " . . Sung by EVELYN LAYE and ENSEMBLE

"Rendezvous" Theatre Suppers, 3/6

44 DEAN STREET, SOHO.

OPERA GLASSES MAY BE HIRED FROM THE THEATRE ATTENDANTS.

Clifton Webb and the Dolly Sisters

Trini

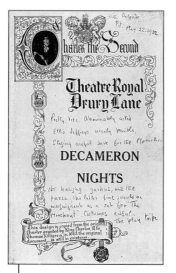

'With Delgado. Pit.

Pretty dire. Abominably acted. Ellis Jeffreys nearly possible. Staging awful save for the Monastery, the hanging gardens, and the piazza; the latter fine; would be magnificent as a set for "The Merchant". Costumes awful, the play tripe.'

'Dire' and 'tripe' it may have been, but the theatre-going public loved it, and it ran for 341 performances.

Ellis Jeffreys as Lady Violante
H.A. Saintsbury as Ricciardo

DECAMERON NIGHTS by Robert McLaughlin
Adapted (with Lyrics) by Boyle Lawrence. Music composed by Herman Finck

The Hanging Gardens

Theatre Royal, Drury Lane

| Managing Directors | ... | ALFRED BUTT and ARTHUR COLLINS |
| Business Manager | ... | M. E. BENJAMIN |

Every evening at 8
Doors open 7.30

Matinées : Wednesday, Thursday and Saturday at 2.15
Doors open 1.45

Decameron Nights

A Romantic Play

in a Prologue and Three Acts

CAST
In the order in which they speak

The LADY FIAMETTA		Miss WINIFRED DAVIS
NERISSA		Miss EVE LYNN
SIMONETTA	(Ladies Exiled	Miss KITTY CADWELL
GRISELDA	from	Miss MABEL FENWICK
OLIVIA	Florence)	Miss MARJORIE WILSON
LAURETTA		Miss KITTY ALLEN
FILOMENA		Miss NITA MAY
EMILIA		Miss KATHLYN CLIFFORD
The NOBLE RICCIARDO LIBERATI	(A Venetian Nobleman)	Mr. H. A. SAINTSBURY
AMATO	(A Friar)	Mr. HORACE CORBYN
BESSANO	(The Abbot of the Monastery)	Mr. ARTHUR LEWIS
The NOBLE TORELLO d'ISTRIA	(A Venetian Nobleman)	Mr. HUGH BUCKLER
SALADIN	(Prince of Damascus)	Mr. COWLEY WRIGHT
IMLIFF	(His Henchman)	Mr. DAVID MILLER
PERDITA	(The Lost One)	Miss WILETTE KERSHAW
MURILLO	(A Friar)	Mr. REGINALD ADAMS

[P.T.O.]

Hugh Buckler as Torello D'Istria

DECAMERON NIGHTS by Robert McLaughlin
Adapted (with Lyrics) by Boyle Lawrence. Music composed by Herman Finck

Margaret Bannerman as Perdita

'**With Mother. Dress Circle. First night of the revival.**

Very interesting to see this famously sensational play; it is far more dramatic and less dated than I had thought from reading it.

Miss Cooper really fine, except for bursts of commonness and mannerisms once or twice. The rest of her company entirely adequate - though I am not sure about Molly Kerr - with the notably strange exception of Fay Davis, who is amazingly bad. I think Gladys Cooper is a really good dramatic actress, and with such a precedent as Mrs Campbell quite amazingly successful and effective.'

'Mrs Tank', as Shaw called her, first appeared at the St James's Theatre in 1893, played by Mrs Patrick Campbell. The play's theme of the sexual double standards of late Victorian England gave both Pinero and Mrs Pat a sensational success.

Gladys Cooper was one of the most beautiful and most photographed women of the period. She began her career as a chorus girl but joined George Alexander's company at the St James's Theatre when she was 22 and quickly established herself as a 'straight' actress. Her performance as Paula Tanqueray was a great personal success, and she later took over the management of the Playhouse Theatre. Her last stage appearance was in 'The Chalk Garden' at the Haymarket in 1971, the year of her death.

John Gielgud left Lady Benson's school in the summer of 1922 and in the autumn was employed by his second cousin, Phyllis Neilson-Terry, to play a small part and ASM in a touring production of 'The Wheel' by J.B. Fagan which she had recently staged in London. At the beginning of 1923 he passed the entrance to the Academy of Dramatic Art (now RADA).

Gladys Cooper as Paula Tanqueray

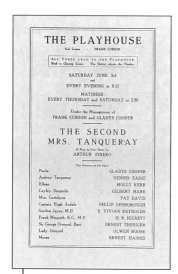

Glayds Cooper as Paula Tanqueray
Denis Eadie as Aubrey Tanqueray

Glayds Cooper as Paula Tanqueray
Molly Kerr as Ellean

Philip Desborough as Capt. Hugh Ardale
Glayds Cooper as Paula Tanqueray

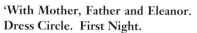

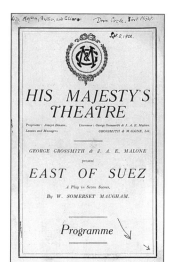

'With Mother, Father and Eleanor. Dress Circle. First Night.

A hard play to criticize. Badly written, the scenes loosely strung together, and the interest constantly shifting; the writing is on the whole bad and faulty. The whole is much too long.

The production (scenery and dresses etc) perfect - but too much - mostly unnecessary, for all its beauty. Though one almost forgives, one resents the holding up of the action - notably in the wedding bit and the first scene.

The acting is on the whole rather good. Rathbone and Marie Ault excellent - also Kendall in a small part. Keen has little to do and is not very remarkably good. France, who ought to my mind, to be the moving spirit of the play, is good in what he has, but has little to do.

Miss Albanesi is wonderful in the last scene, which I found (theatrically) perfect, but her personality is not alluring enough to carry off the whole play. She lacks allurement - and her gesture is faulty. Above all - she repeats her effects very much too often - needs very much more variety - but here her part is considerably at fault.

I shall hope to see it again one day, with considerable cuts and no first night anxiety.'

Basil Dean was one of the most influential figures in the British theatre in the first half of the century. Beginning as an actor he was instrumental in setting up the Liverpool Repertory Theatre. With Alec L. Rea he set up the ReandeaN production company, presenting many successful London shows, and in the Second World War was the founder and first director of the Entertainments National Service Association (ENSA). As a director, he had a reputation as a perfectionist and a martinet, but he had a knowledge and understanding of the technical side of theatre (especially lighting) which always made his presentations of great visual interest.

His production of 'East of Suez' spared no effort or expense in achieving Pekingese authenticity, even to the extent of struggling with the actors' trade union to retain his 'real' Chinese supers rather than have 'yellowed-up' union members.

Meggie Albanesi was the bright, young, rising star of the English theatre who died of peritonitis at the age of 24; this was her penultimate stage appearance.

'Her beautiful acting always delighted me - especially as the daughter in Clemence Dane's 'A Bill of Divorcement' (afterwards played for the screen by John Barrymore and Katharine Hepburn.)

I saw her also in 'Reparation' with Henry Ainley (a stage version of Tolstoy's 'Living Corpse') and in her last stage appearance 'The Lilies of the Field' by John Hastings Turner.

J.G.,1993

Malcolm Keen as Henry Anderson
Meggie Albanesi as Daisy
Marie Ault as Amah

31

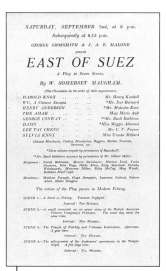

SATURDAY, SEPTEMBER 2nd, at 8 p.m.

Subsequently at 8.15 p.m.

GEORGE GROSSMITH & J. A. E. MALONE

present

EAST OF SUEZ

A Play in Seven Scenes.

By W. SOMERSET MAUGHAM.

(The Characters in the order of their appearance).

HAROLD KNOX	Mr. Henry Kendall
WU, A Chinese Servant	*Mr. Ivor Barnard
HENRY ANDERSON	*Mr. Malcolm Keen
THE AMAH	Miss Marie Ault
GEORGE CONWAY	**Mr. Basil Rathbone
DAISY	*Miss Meggie Albanesi
LEE TAI CHENG	Mr. C. V. France
SYLVIA KNOX	Miss Ursula Millard

Chinese Merchants, Coolies, Mandarins, Beggars, Monks, Tourists, Servants, etc.

*These artistes appear by permission of BeawdoN.

**Mr. Basil Rathbone appears by permission of Mr. Gilbert Miller.

Mesdames : Norah Robinson, Mercia Swinburne, Marian Lind, Yorke Stephens, Rita Page, Hilda Moss, Kitty Marshall, Dorothy Wordsworth, Maureen Dillon, Kitty McCoy, May Wardx, Kathleen MacVeagh.

Messieurs : Matthew Forsyth, Hugh Dempster, Laurence Ireland, Osborn Adair, Sholto Douglas.

The action of the Play passes in Modern Peking.

SCENE 1.—A Street in Peking. Towards Nightfall.

Interval : Two Minutes.

SCENE 2.—A small verandah on an upper story of the British American Tobacco Company's Premises. The same day about the same time.

Interval : Two Minutes.

SCENE 3.—The Temple of Fidelity and Virtuous Inclination. Afternoon. A year later.

Interval : Ten Minutes.

SCENE 4.—The sitting-room of the Andersons' apartments in the Temple. Night. A few days later.

Interval : Ten Minutes.

C.V. France as Lee Tai Cheng

A street in Peking

Meggie Albanesi as Daisy

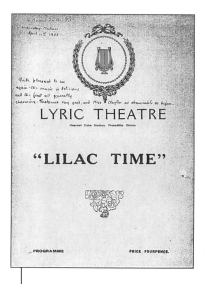

'First visit. With Angus and his mother. In the stalls.

A most charming and delightful first act gave unfair hopes of what afterwards proved a most indifferent entertainment. The music is of course beautiful, but the secondary 'plot' which occupies the last two acts is melodramatic and silly. Everyone struggled with it, and on the whole it was excellently played and sung, except by Doris Clayton, who made a silly part hopelessly bad by overacting and badly acting. [Edmund] Gwenn brilliant but wasted.'

Second visit 11 April 1923.

'With Angus. In the Pit.

Quite pleasant to see again - the music is delicious and the first act generally charming. Baskcomb very good, and Miss Clayton as abominable as before.'

'Lilac Time' had opened in December 1922 and ran until June 1924. A.W. Baskcomb took over from Edmund Gwenn in the part of Christian Veit. A great success and revived many times, its popularity derived largely from Schubert's melodies and a somewhat idealised Vienna situated nearer Arcadia than Austria. The unfortunate Miss Clayton next appeared as Abdallah, Captain of Thieves, in the Lyceum pantomime 'The Forty Thieves' at the Lyceum in 1924, and subsequently disappeared without trace.

Act 1 - Courtyard of a house in Vienna

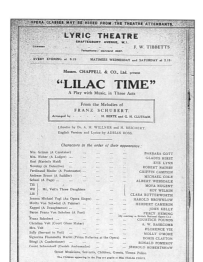

OPERA GLASSES MAY BE HIRED FROM THE THEATRE ATTENDANTS.

LYRIC THEATRE

SHAFTESBURY AVENUE, W.1.

Licensee ... ... F. W. TIBBETTS

Telephone : Gerrard 3037.

EVERY EVENING at 8.15   MATINEES WEDNESDAY and SATURDAY at 2.15

Messrs. CHAPPELL & CO., Ltd. present

"LILAC TIME"

A Play with Music, in Three Acts

From the Melodies of
FRANZ SCHUBERT.

Arranged by ... ... H. BERTE and G. H. CLUTSAM.

Libretto by Dr. A. M. WILLNER and H. REICHERT.
English Version and Lyrics by ADRIAN ROSS.

Characters in the order of their appearance :

Mrs. Grimm (A Caretaker)	BARBARA GOTT
Mrs. Weber (A Lodger)	GLADYS HIRST
Rosi (Marini's Maid)	EVE LYNN
Novotny (A Detective)	ROBERT NAINBY
Ferdinand Binder (A Postmaster)	GRIFFIN CAMPION
Andreas Braun (A Saddler)	MICHAEL COLE
Schani (A Page)	ALBERT WEBSDALE
Tilli ⎫	MOYA NUGENT
Willi ⎬ Mr. Veit's Three Daughters ...	ROY WILSON
Lili ⎭	CLARA BUTTERWORTH
Joanna Michael Vogl (An Opera Singer) ...	HAROLD BROWNLOW
Moritz Von Schwind (A Painter)	HERBERT CAMERON
Kappel (A Draughtsman)	JOHN KELLY
Baron Franz Von Schober (A Poet)	PERCY HEMING
	(by courtesy in British National Opera Co.)
Franz Schubert	COURTICE POUNDS
Christian Veit (Court Glass Maker)	A. W. BASKCOMB
Mrs. Veit	FLORENCE VIE
Sally (Servant to Veit)	MOLLY O'MORE
Signorina Flammetta Marini (Prima Ballerina at the Opera) ...	DORIS CLAYTON
Stingl (A Confectioner)	RONALD POMEROY
Count Scharntorff (Danish Ambassador) ...	JERROLD ROBERTSHAW

Street Musicians, Servants, Children, Guests, Vienna Police.

The Children appearing in the Play are pupils at Miss ITALIA CONTI.

AFTERNOON TEA.—A Special Service of Tea is served at Matinees in all the Saloons

LILAC TIME
From the melodies of Franz Schubert, arranged by H. Berte and G.H. Clutsam

Above and below: scenes from Lilac Time

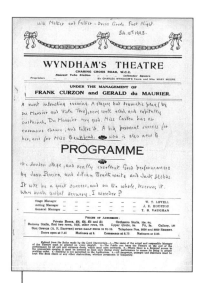

'**With Mother and Father. First Night.**

A most interesting evening. A stagey but dramatic play (by du Maurier and Viola Tree), very well acted and capitally sustained. Du Maurier very good. Miss Carten has an enormous chance and takes it. A big personal success for her, and for Miss Bankhead, who is also new to the London stage, and really excellent. Good performances by Joan Pereira and Lilian Braithwaite and Jack Hobbs. It will be a great success, and on the whole, deserves it. Why such awful scenery, I wonder?'

Gerald du Maurier, the son of George du Maurier, famous 'Punch' artist and author of 'Trilby', was knighted in 1922 and regarded as one of the leaders of his profession. Although lacking the traditional assets of the leading actor - good looks, fine voice - he nevertheless remained one of the most popular actors of his generation. His so-called 'naturalness' was to be a powerful influence on younger actors, including Laurence Olivier.

Du Maurier had obviously written a good part for himself and the play ran for the best part of a year. Audrey Carten made a great personal success but only appeared on stage a few more times before apparently giving up acting in favour of writing not very successful plays with her sister, Waveney. Miss Bankhead, of course, went on to become Tallulah.

Caricature of Tallulah Banhead and Gerald du Maurier

Audrey Carten as Una Lowry

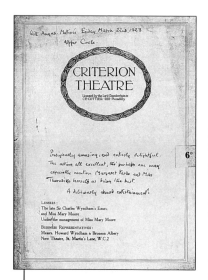

'With Angus. Matinée.
Dress Circle.

Prodigiously amusing, and entirely delightful. The acting all excellent, tho' perhaps one may especially mention Margaret Yarde and Miss Thorndike as being the best.

A deliciously absurd entertainment.'

Sybil Thorndike's long career and her great personal gifts of vitality, generosity, diligence and modesty made her one of the most loved figures in theatre throughout her life. She had come to the Academy of Dramatic Art the previous year and rehearsed Gielgud's class in scenes from 'Medea'. With her husband, Lewis Casson, she formed a partnership in the theatre and in life which sometimes failed, often succeeded, occasionally touched greatness and never ever gave up. Their last appearance together was in 1963 when they went on tour with a play called 'Queen B': she was 82 and he 88.

Gielgud's note is a useful reminder that although more often thought of as a player of tragedy and Grand Guignol, Sybil Thorndike could also turn her hand to lighter material with great success.

'Though she was inclined to overact in comedy, and was always the first to admit it.

I directed her in 'Treasure Hunt' in which she was inimitably funny, and acted with her in 'A Day by the Sea' by N.C. Hunter in which she gave one of her most beautiful performances in a straight part.'

J.G.,1993

ADVERTISING APRIL
or, The Girl who made the Sunshine Jealous
by Herbert Farjeon and Horace Horsnell

Sybil Thorndike as April Mawne

THE MAGAZINE-PROGRAMME
(TITLE REGISTERED)

With Angus. Dress Circle.
First Night. April 11th 1923

Strand Theatre
LONDON

Proprietor Jonl. G. Levy.
Sole Lessee and Manager - - ARTHUR BOURCHIER.

A very fine play, sordid,
but intensely dramatic,
perfectly acted by
its three or four
characters.

Only comparable with
Jane Clegg" - a really
good drama.

CHARLES B. COCHRAN

Miss Lord really wonderful, but perhaps no better than Marion—

In association with ARTHUR HOPKINS

PAULINE LORD

The only thing I disliked were the soliloquies in the last act, which seemed out of the atmosphere altogeth—

"ANNA CHRISTIE"
by
EUGENE O'NEILL

Programme

SEE THE THEATRICAL COMPETITION ON PAGE 19.

'With Angus. Dress Circle.
First Night.

A very fine play, sordid but intensely dramatic, perfectly acted by its three or four characters.

Only comparable with "Jane Clegg" - a really good drama. Miss Lord really wonderful, but perhaps no better than [George] Marion - the only thing I disliked were the soliloquies in the last act, which seemed out of the atmosphere altogether.'

A matinée of 'Lilac Time' followed by the first night of 'Anna Christie' says much for Gielgud's hunger for the variety of theatrical experience which characterises his young theatre-going. O'Neill's plays had been introduced to London audiences by the enterprising Norman MacDermott at the Everyman Theatre, Hampstead, but this was the first West End production of any of his plays; it ran for a respectable 103 performances.

Pauline Lord was an American by birth. Many critics hailed her as a great actress following her performance in this play; she returned to America the next year and, as far as can be traced, never again appeared on the London stage.

GEORGE
MARION
AS
CHRISTOPHERSON

FRANK SHANNON
AS MAT

PAULINE LORD
AS ANNA

STRAND THEATRE
STRAND W.C.F.

Box Office. Telephone: GERRARD 2830.

EVERY EVENING AT 8.30.

MATINEES : WEDNESDAY AND SATURDAY AT 2.30.

CHARLES B. COCHRAN

Presents

In association with ARTHUR HOPKINS

PAULINE LORD

In EUGENE O'NEILL'S Play

"ANNA CHRISTIE"

With

GEORGE MARION and FRANK SHANNON

Settings by ROBERT EDMOND JONES

Staged by ARTHUR HOPKINS

Characters in the order in which they appear :

Johnny-the-Priest	JAMES C. MACK
First Longshoreman ..	G. O. TAYLOR
Second Longshoreman ..	EDDY REED
Larry	EUGENE LINCOLN
A Potman	ARTHUR HURLEY
Chris Christopherson ..	GEORGE MARION
Marthy Owen	MILDRED BEVERLY
Anna Christopherson ..	PAULINE LORD
Mat Burke	FRANK SHANNON
Johnson	OLE ANDERSON
Three Sailors A. REILLY, C. HANSEN and B. KENNEDY

SEE THE THEATRICAL COMPETITION ON PAGE 19.

Pauline Lord
as Anna
Christopherson

ANNA CHRISTIE by Eugene O'Neill

OUR CAPTIOUS CRITIC.

"ANNA CHRISTIE" AT THE STRAND THEATRE.

THERE seems to be a spell put upon America which prevents her writing a "classic." Perhaps the pocket bulks too largely in the minds of her people, making figures like Rockefeller and Carnegie the gods of the race, so that the people themselves, who should be the sole vision of the writer, are only half seen while his attention is drawn towards the idol named Success. However that may be, you feel that if America had not been America Mr. Eugene O'Neill might have made a classic of "Anna Christie."

But as it is the hardness of the United States is over it all.

There are only four characters of any moment. As to the unfortunate Anna herself, you feel that she wishes to marry Mat Burke to get a home—not because she loves and yearns to be loved. Mat Burke, the stoker, with his egotism and his fanaticism, lies too near madness for epic use, while the other pair, Anna's father and that father's "woman," though human, are too subdued in tone to lift the drama against the influence of the more predominant daughter and her lover, to the normal and attractive level on which enduring work must stand.

Nothing could be more admirable than the genuine, straightforward way in which this telling play is both written and acted. Not for one second do we hear a word, or observe a gesture, which is meant to gain applause merely for its own little sake. From the moment when the demoralised Anna, returning to her drunken father after his neglect of her since she was a child of five, stealthily reveals to us what sort of damaged goods she has become, right on to the end of the play, no attempt is made to refine the picture of these seafaring people. The daughter, rescued from the clutches of a sailors' brothel to the comparative security of a home on her father's barge, shows no fondness for her father or worship of her lover. The author is out for the real thing, and we see not an angel but a woman who would have been about as good as others had she had their chances. Chris, the father, remains the weak fuddler he has been all his life, or at least is ready to seek refuge in drink as soon as trouble comes—this case when he learns of his daughter's past. Mat Burke, the ship's stoker who wants to marry Anna, seems as ready to swear oaths to his God as to crack human heads, while the fourth character in the drama, Chris's "woman," Marthy Brown, though she rather heroically clears off the barge to make way for the supposed Miss Purity who is coming to keep house there, cannot restrain a hard, abrupt laugh of derision on finding out how soiled are the wings of this supposedly snow-white dove.

From beginning to end there is no concession to sentiment or ideality. Chris is no Dan'l Peggotty and Mat Burke no Ham.

Plays of this kind, in order to succeed, must be written and acted by the best authors and actors, because before satisfying their audience they have to oppose the instinct of the public for something of more refinement and charm. In "Anna Christie" these requirements are met both by the writer of the play and the theatrical company at the Strand Theatre. At the head of this company stands Miss Pauline Lord, as Anna. She has that sing-song and rather sentimental note in her voice which is found in most American stage performers, but apart from this her utterance is moving, her varied gestures are as subtle as they are effective, and her general acting of a fine, free dramatic order. It is altogether an impressive performance, though the limited range of the character of Anna renders it necessary to see Miss Lord in other parts of a different kind before indulging in superlatives of the all-round variety. In harmony with her performance is the study of Anna's weak-minded and tipsy father, Chris Christopherson, by Mr. George Marion, though you are doubtful in your mind as to the thorough illusion of his intoxication. This is often the case on the stage, and makes one wonder if actors are afraid of getting so drunk mentally through over-realisation of their character that they fear the detail business of acting their part would suffer if they went "all out" for it. Chris had neglected his wife and child during his voyages over the seas of the world, and had now come to curse "that old devil sea" for the toll it had taken of his relatives. Hence his wrath at finding that Anna has taken up with an ocean-going stoker instead of settling down with an inland man. This wild stoker, who is always calling on God to stiffen one person or to help another, is no credit to the play; and at critical moments Mr. Frank Shannon rather fails to keep the acting of the character up to the level attained by Miss Pauline Lord and Mr. George Marion. Miss Mildred Beverly is perfect as Marthy Owen, a part of no great difficulty. Taken altogether, we are the richer for seeing such a play as this with such a leading lady.

The first act of "Anna Christie" takes place in a New York public-house, and the rest of the play also maintains a pleasant social intercourse with alcohol. So it cannot represent the America of to-day—at least, within the three-mile limit. Should the piece have a long run it will prove that clothes are not always the thing, for there will be no rage set in to copy Anna's frocks or Marthy's hat, or Chris's neckwear. Nor would the announcement "Barge suite by ——" set furniture hunters running to ——West End emporium to secure a similar set for their morning rooms.

Towards the end the drama halts and plays weakly with a knife and a pistol, important episodes ineptly introduced by an author who is able to get all the tragedy he wants in words alone.

And now we are looking forward to the next O'Neill play, hoping that London will see it soon.

ANNA'S FATHER, WITH HIS LAND LEGS ON · GEORGE MARION

THEY ALL WANT TO SETTLE DOWN QUIETLY, THEY HAVE A CHAT ABOUT IT

PAULINE LORD, GEORGE MARION & FRANK SHANNON.

FROM AMERICA—BUT ON "IT AIN'T DRY."

'With Father. In the Dress Circle. First Night.

Intensely interesting, and the second and third acts magnificent. The last appears to me much doctored from the original. Anyway, it fails badly and is not well acted. Otherwise quite the most wonderful and original play I have seen for some time. Rathbone, France, and Wills are all good, and Frances Carson very excellent. Ada King, Banks and Mollison gave superb performances. A maddening audience giggled at moments but the play seemed to be appreciated by the majority. It will be most intriguing to see if it is a success.'

'It was not - but ran about twice as long as "The Insect Play" and "Robots" became the fashionable slang for a few weeks.'

J.G.,1993

Capek's play must have come as quite a shock, dealing as it did with the idea of world domination by man-made machines in 1950, and although it may not have attracted the groundlings, it ran for about four months. 'Robots', of course, have stayed with us much longer.

In May of this year, Gielgud was seen by Nigel Playfair in an ADA production of 'The Admirable Crichton', in which he played the silly ass, Woolley, in the first two acts and Crichton himself in the last two. As a result of this, Playfair offered Gielgud the part of Felix, the Poet Butterfly in 'The Insect Play', which Karel Capek wrote with his brother Josef, and which Playfair produced at the Regent Theatre. The production was not a success and ran for only six weeks. In spite of this failure, Playfair re-engaged several of the cast, including Gielgud, for his production of John Drinkwater's new play 'Robert E. Lee', which opened at the Regent in June.

R.U.R. (Rossum's Universal Robots) by Karel Čapek.
Translated by Paul Selver. Adapted by Nigel Playfair

Leslie Banks as Radius

ST·MARTIN'S·THEATRE
LONDON
LESSEE   MANAGERS
B·A·MEYER·   REANDEAN·LTD

R. U. R.
(Rossum's Universal Robots)
A Fantastic Melodrama
By KAREL CAPEK.
Translated by PAUL SELVER.   Adapted by NIGEL PLAYFAIR.

THE CHARACTERS IN THE ORDER OF THEIR APPEARANCE

Harry Domain *(General Manager of Rossum's Universal Robots)* By Mr. Basil Rathbone
                                                   (By permission of Mr. Gilbert Miller)
Sulla *(a Robotess)* .. .. .. ,, Miss Beatrix Thomson
Marius *(a Robot)* .. .. .. ,, Mr. Gilbert Ritchie
Helena Glory .. .. .. ,, Miss Frances Carson
Dr. Gall *(Head of the Physiological and Experimental Department of R.U.R.)* ,, Mr. Charles V. France
Mr. Alquist *(Head of the Works Department of R.U.R.)* ,, Mr. Brember Wills
Jacob Berman *(Chief Cashier for R.U.R.)* .. ,, Mr. Clifford Mollison
Emma .. .. ,, Miss Ada King
Radius *(a Robot)* .. .. .. ,, Mr. Leslie Banks
Helena *(a Robotess)* .. .. .. ,, Miss Olga Lindo
Primus *(a Robot)* .. .. .. ,, Mr. Ian Hunter
Robots .. Messrs. Austin Trevor, Leslie Perrins, Alan Howland, Charles Cornock, Roy Leaker, Hugh Williams, George Cowley, Hugh Sinclair, Ernest Digges, John F. Barham, Geoffrey Dunlop, Frederick Fauton, Cyril McLaglan, Cresswell Garth.

A Robot

Frances Carson as Helena Glory, Basil Rathbone as Domain

Leslie Banks as Radius
Frances Carson as Helena Glory

ACT I. Domain's Room in the Offices of Rossum's
Universal Robots.
Here there will be an interval of ten minutes.

ACT II. Helena's Drawing-Room. Ten years later.
Morning.
Here there will be an interval of ten minutes.

ACT III. The Same. Towards Sundown.
After Act III. there will be an interval of five minutes only.

ACT IV. A Laboratory. One year later.

Place : An Island.   Time : The Future.

❖ ❖ ❖

The production devised by BASIL DEAN.

The semi-permanent scenery designed by GEORGE W. HARRIS.

The imaginative costumes of the Robots made by Messrs. B. J. SIMMONS
of Covent Garden, from designs by GEORGE W. HARRIS.

Miss Frances Carson's dresses by BERTHE, of Half Moon Street; her
hat by ZYROT.

Chemical Apparatus and Microscope used in the Fourth Act kindly lent by
Messrs. R. B. TURNER & Co., Eagle Street, W.C.

Electrical Research Apparatus by the General Electric Company.

The Play presented by arrangement with the Directors of the Lyric Theatre,
Hammersmith.

9

Brember Wills as Mr Alquist
Olga Lindo as Helena, a Robotess
Ian Hunter as Primus, a robot

R.U.R. (Rossum's Universal Robots) by Karel Čapek.
Translated by Paul Selver. Adapted by Nigel Playfair

Beatrix Thomson as Sulla, a robotess
Frances Carson as Helena Glory

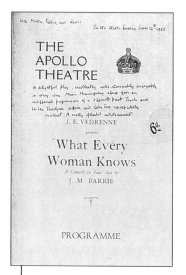

THE
APOLLO
THEATRE

A delightful play, excellently acted, thoroughly enjoyable in every way. Marie Hemingway alone gave an indifferent performance of a difficult part. Hilda Trevelyan superb, and Lady Tree unexpectedly excellent. A really splendid entertainment.

J. E. VEDRENNE

presents

What Every
Woman Knows

A Comedy in Four Acts by
J. M. BARRIE

PROGRAMME

6d.

'With Mother, Father and Lewis. In the stalls.

A delightful play, excellently acted, thoroughly enjoyable in every way. Marie Hemingway alone gave an indifferent performance of a difficult part. Tearle good, Hilda Trevelyan superb and Lady Tree unexpectedly excellent. A really splendid entertainment.'

Barrie's variation on 'behind every successful man...' was first produced in 1908 at the Duke of York's. Hilda Trevelyan (Maggie Wylie) was one of four members of the original cast who appeared in this revival. She was the original Wendy in 'Peter Pan' and played the part over nine hundred times as well as appearing in a number of Barrie's other plays.

Godfrey Tearle, who was knighted in 1951, had a distinguished career in the theatre, his Antony and Othello being particularly memorable. Lady Tree, the widow of Sir Herbert Beerhohm Tree, continued to work in the theatre until two years before her death at the age of 78.

*Scene from the 1908 production
with Hilda Trevelyan as Maggie Wylie*

Godfrey Tearle as John Shand
Marie Hemingway as Lady Sybil Tenterden

Hilda Trevelyan as Maggie Wylie

*Henry Vibart, Frank Pettingell, Norman MacOwan
and Geoffrey Tearle*

Godfrey Tearle as John Shand
Hilda Trevelyan as Maggie Wylie

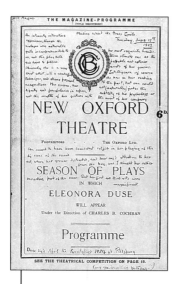

'With Angus. Standing behind the Dress Circle.

An intensely interesting experience, though the dialogue was naturally quite incomprehensible to us, and the play dull and hard to follow. Obviously she is a very great artist, with a wonderful technique, and strong personal magnetism. Her reserve, her dignity and forcefulness in repose, and the wealth of her gesture with her most exquisite hands - these struck one as the palpable and exterior assets of her genius. Intelligence of course she has in her reading of the part, but one could not (naturally) judge the subtlety of her psychology or the merit of her company.

She seemed to be somewhat selfish in her playing of the big scene of the second act, where her groans distracted, and drew one's attention to her from the boy, and I thought her rather overacting part of the scene. But her first and third acts were magnificent.'

Later Note:
'Duse died April the twenty-first 1924 at Pittsburg (my grandmother's birthday!)'

The legendary Italian actress obviously lived up to her reputation, though she had already appeared in London several times. In 1928 Gielgud found himself appearing as Oswald ('the boy') with perhaps an even more formidable Mrs Alving in Mrs Patrick Campbell.

Portrait of Eleanor Duse

'With Angus, Philip and Charles. Roving. The coloured people excellent in every way - Florence Mills particularly admirable - the English revue very indifferent - tho' Odette Myrtil occasionally pleased us - but the comparison was more than odious.

'With Angus, Philip and Charles. Roving.

The coloured people excellent in every way - Florence Mills particularly admirable - the English revue very indifferent - tho' Odette Myrtil occasionally pleased us - but the comparison was more than odious.'

This was the first appearance in London of the tiny Florence Mills, a brilliant dancer and singer. She died in New York in 1927 at the tragically early age of 26; ten thousand people filed past her body in Harlem. The grand-daughter of a slave, she believed strongly in equal rights for black Americans and, while in London, often visited the Embankment and the East End, giving money to the needy people she met.

Florence Mills

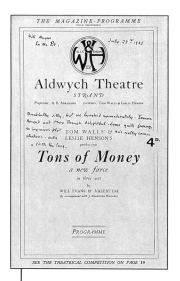

THE MAGAZINE-PROGRAMME

Aldwych Theatre
STRAND
Proprietor: A. E. ABRAHAMS   Licensees: TOM WALLS & LESLIE HENSON

TOM WALLS' & LESLIE HENSON'S   **4**D.
production

Tons of Money
a new farce
in three acts

by
WILL EVANS & VALENTINE
(By arrangement with J. HASTINGS HOWARD)

PROGRAMME

SEE THE THEATRICAL COMPETITION ON PAGE 19

'With Angus. In the Pit.

Dreadfully silly, but we laughed immoderately. Yvonne Arnaud and Mary Brough delightful - Lynn quite funny. An ingenious plot and really comic situations - only a little too long.'

Tom Walls was a fairly successful musical comedy performer when he went into partnership with Leslie Henson to produce 'Tons of Money' at the Shaftesbury Theatre in 1922. The play was a huge success and transferred to the Aldwych, at which theatre Walls was to continue his success with the famous Aldwych farces, many of them by Ben Travers, such as 'Rookery Nook', 'Plunder' and 'Thark'.

Mary Brough and Ralph Lynn appeared in many of the Aldwych plays; Yvonne Arnaud was born in France and began her career as a child pianist but had a long and successful career in British theatre and films.

'In 'Tons of Money', Yvonne had a catchphrase 'Aubrey, I have an idea' and I can still hear the witty way she used it.

She was to play brilliantly as Mrs Frail in my production of Congreve's "Love for Love" at the Phoenix and Haymarket theatres in 1944.'

J.G.,1993

Yvonne Arnaud (L) as Louise Allington
Ena Mason (C) as Simpson
Ralph Lynn (R) as Aubrey Allington

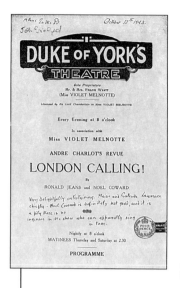

'Stood with Angus. In the Pit. First performance.

When pruned of the three or four poor items, it will be a really excellent show - Maisie Gay is magnificent - and Gertrude Lawrence very good - Coward will be better when he is less nervous - but he's a little ineffectual and amateurish at present. Edlin quite funny - some very good scenes - but it all suffered from the nervous slowness of the players today and the inordinate length of the programme, which will of course be cut.'

Later visit. 12 October 1923.

'Alone. In the Pit.

Very delightfully entertaining. Maisie [Gay] and Gertrude Lawrence chiefly - Noël Coward is definitely not good, and it is a pity there is no ingénue in the show who can apparently sing in tune.'

One of André Charlot's many revues, but perhaps most notable as the first occasion on which the adult Coward and Gertrude Lawrence appeared together on stage. By the time of Gielgud's second visit, the show had been shortened by one item; Coward's satirical sketch based on the Sitwells, entitled 'The Swiss Family Whittlebot', was retained, however.

Maisie Gay was an extremely popular character comedienne, whose most famous creation was the loveable Cockney charlady, Mrs 'Arris. Osteo-arthritis forced her to retire from the stage in 1932.

Gertude Lawrence and Nöel Coward

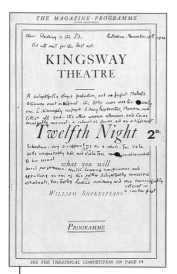

'Alone. Standing in the Pit. Did not wait for the last act.

A delightfully staged production, and a perfect Malvolio. Otherwise most indifferent - the letter scene was the only one I thoroughly enjoyed. Sydney Fairbrother, Hannen, and Cellier all good - the other women atrocious, and Caine dreadfully miscast - a colourless Orsino and an indifferent Sebastian - very disappointing as a whole. The Viola quite unspeakably bad, and Viola Tree condescended to her usual bored performance. Noëlle Sonning conspicuous and appalling as one of the rather delightfully conceived attendants, Vere Turley [Turleigh] looked ravishing and was successfully reticent in a similar part.'

Baliol Holloway (Malvolio) is a neglected figure in twentieth century Shakespearean acting. A member of Sir Frank Benson's company of players and sportsmen, he went on to become a leading actor at Stratford-upon-Avon and the Old Vic and played practically every leading part in Shakespeare. J.C. Trewin, that great and generous Shakespearean critic, rated his Richard III on a par with Olivier's and his Cassius as good as Gielgud's.

Nicholas Hannen (Andrew Aguecheek) was a versatile and stylish actor, known in the theatre as 'Beau' and married to Athene Seyler. He was awarded the O.B.E. (Mil.) for his Army service in World War I and appeared with distinction in many classical and contemporary plays. Sydney Fairbrother (Maria) was one of that great line of comic character actresses who graced many London productions and British films for many years. Frank Cellier (Sir Toby Belch) learnt his trade with William Poel and touring productions of Shakespeare before becoming a regular and reliable supporting actor in the West End.

The producer, Donald Calthrop, was a reasonably

successful actor who occasionally ventured into management. The critics were generally impressed by the simplicity and clarity of this production, although his next presentation of 'A Midsummer's Night Dream' was nowhere near as well received.

'Calthrop sent for me to his office after seeing me play a scene from Hotspur at the RADA (directed by Claude Rains). He told me my name was impossible for the theatre and that I ought to change it.

Though tempted to use my Terry connection (as my aunt Mabel Terry Lewis had done, and also Phyllis and Dennis Neilson-Terry) I somehow determined to keep my own name. "People may not know how to pronounce it," I declared, "but it looks so odd that I think they may remember it."'

J.G.,1993

Cartoon of Frank Cellier as Sir Toby Belch
Nicholas Hannen as Sir Andrew Aguecheek

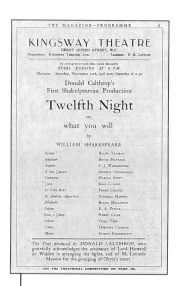

THE MAGAZINE—PROGRAMME 9

KINGSWAY THEATRE
GREAT QUEEN STREET, W.C.
Proprietors : KINGSWAY THEATRE, LTD.   Licensee : F. R. LITTLER

By arrangement with Miss Lillah McCarthy
EVERY EVENING AT 8 P.M.
Matinées : Saturday, November 10th, and every Saturday at 2.30

Donald Calthrop's
First Shakespearean Production

Twelfth Night
or,
what you will
by
WILLIAM SHAKESPEARE

Orsino	RALPH TRUMAN
Sebastian	BRUCE BELFRAGE
Antonio	S. J. WARMINGTON
A Sea Captain	ANDREW CHURCHMAN
Valentine	HAROLD SCOTT
Curio	BASIL CUNARD
Sir Toby Belch	FRANK CELLIER
Sir Andrew Aguecheek	NICHOLAS HANNEN
Malvolio	BALIOL HOLLOWAY
Fabian	B. A. PITTAR
Feste, a Clown	HENRY CAINE
Olivia	VIOLA TREE
Viola	DOROTHY CHESTON
Maria	SYDNEY FAIRBROTHER

The Play produced by DONALD CALTHROP, who
gratefully acknowledges the assistance of Lord Howard
de Walden in arranging the fights, and of M. Leonide
Massine for the grouping of Olivia's court.

SEE THE THEATRICAL COMPETITION ON PAGE 19.

*Probably B.A. Pittar as Fabian
Nicholas Hannen
as Sir Andrew Aguecheek
Frank Cellier as Sir Toby Belch
Sydney Fairbrother (below) as Maria*

Frank Cellier as Sir Toby Belch
Sydney Fairbrother as Maria

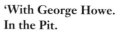

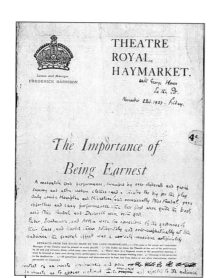

'With George Howe.
In the Pit.

A moderately good performance, swamped by over-elaborate and garish scenery and ultra-modern clothes - and a theatre too big for the play. Only Louise Hampton and Nicholson (and occasionally Miss Kendal) gave effortless and easy performances - the two first were quite the best and Miss Kendal and Deverell were both good.

Faber, Scudamore, and Atkin were too conscious of the goodness of their lines, and hurled them deliberately and over-emphatically at the audience - the general effect was a self-conscious artificiality instead of an innate preciousness and pose so innate as to appear natural in the characters and affected to the audience.'

Allan Aynesworth had been the original Algy in 1895; this, his own production, was done in modern dress, but Gielgud's famous 1939 production with Edith Evans eschewed all such novelty. George Howe was a student with Gielgud at the Academy and played Canon Chasuble in his revival of the production in August 1939. Tyrone Guthrie said of Gielgud's production that it 'establishes the high-water mark in the production of artificial comedy in our epoch'.

In December 1923, Gielgud left the Academy of Dramatic Art and played Charley in a Christmas production of 'Charley's Aunt' at the Comedy Theatre. After Christmas he went to meet J.B. Fagan, the author of 'The Wheel' and director of the repertory company at the Oxford Playhouse. 'Fagan was an Irishman of great personal charm. Also he was extremely talented as author, producer, and impresario. His death in Hollywood in 1933 was a real loss to the theatre.' (John Gielgud, 'Early Days'.) Fagan offered him a contract and Gielgud joined the Oxford Playhouse company in January 1924.

Nancy Atkin as Cecily Cardew
John Deverell as Algernon Moncrieff

John Deverell as
Algernon Moncrieff

Leslie Faber (L) as John Worthing
John Deverell (R) as Algernon Moncrieff

'With Mother - In the Stalls.

Edith Evans gave a marvellous performance, really at last worthy of her critics' everlasting praise. Her two big scenes magnificent. Playfair, Norman and Scott good - also Lanchester, Sims, and Green and Taylor. Yarde a trifle Maisie Gay, but very comic indeed. Loraine and Anstruther not v. good, ensemble effect bad.

Not as good an acting play as "Love for Love". Good clothes and Act II set, rest a bit garish.'

Although he was now working at Oxford, Gielgud seems to have taken every opportunity to return to London and catch up with the current theatre scene. The night before this visit to Hammersmith he had been playing Valentine in 'Love for Love' at Oxford.

Gielgud would later work with Edith Evans on a number of occasions, each being an admirer of the other's work. In 1942 Gielgud played Mirabell to her Millamant in one scene from 'The Way of the World' for a charity performance. He directed the play and again played Mirabell in 1953, this time with Pamela Brown as Millamant.

Elsa Lanchester as Peggy

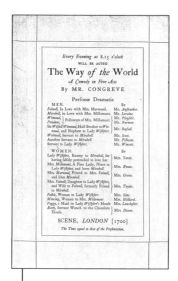

Robert Loraine as Mirabell
Edith Evans as Mrs Millamant

Joyce Kennedy as Mrs Marwood
(Joyce Kennedy took over the part during the run of the play.)

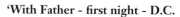

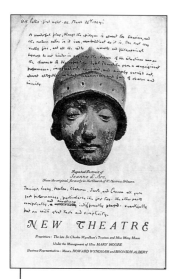

Reputed Portrait of
Jeanne d'Arc,
From the original, formerly in the Church of St Maurice, Orleans

NEW THEATRE

Proprietors: The late Sir Charles Wyndham's Trustees and Miss Mary Moore
Under the Management of Miss MARY MOORE
Business Representatives: Messrs. HOWARD WYNDHAM and BRONSON ALBERY

'With Father - first night - D.C.

A wonderful play, though the epilogue is almost too Shavian, and the modern satire in it jars, even brilliant as it is. The rest was really fine, and all the witty remarks and philosophical byways do not hinder in any way the drama of the situation or the clearness of the exposition. Sybil Thorndike [as Joan] gave a magnificent performance, imaginatively conceived, and simply carried out, almost altogether without mannerism, and full of charm and sincerity.

Thesiger, Leahy, Horton, Clarence, Swete and Casson all gave good performances, particularly the first two - the other parts competently and sometimes indifferently played - beautifully put on with great taste and simplicity.'

Although the first production of the play was in New York the previous year, this was the first British presentation, produced by the author and Sybil Thorndike's husband, Lewis Casson, with designs by Charles Ricketts. Sybil Thorndike's qualities of enthusiasm, sincerity and personal goodness helped make this performance into one of her most memorable.

Joan (Sybil Thorndike) recognises the Dauphin (Ernest Thesiger)

Sybil Thorndike as Joan

WEDNESDAY, MARCH 26th, 1924, at 7.30.

Miss MARY MOORE and Miss SYBIL THORNDIKE
present

SAINT JOAN

A Chronicle Play in Six Scenes and an Epilogue
by
BERNARD SHAW

Characters (*In order of appearance*):

Robert de Baudricourt	SHAYLE GARDNER
Steward	FRANCIS HOPE
Joan	SYBIL THORNDIKE
Bertrand de Poulengey	VICTOR LEWISOHN
The Archbishop of Rheims	ROBERT CUNNINGHAM
La Trémouille, *Constable of France*	BRUCE WINSTON
Court Page	SAM PICKLES
Gilles de Rais, *Bluebeard*	MILTON ROSMER
Captain La Hire	RAYMOND MASSEY
The Dauphin (*later Charles VII*)	ERNEST THESIGER
The Duchesse de la Trémouille	BEATRICE SMITH
Dunois, *Bastard of Orleans*	ROBERT HORTON
Dunois' Page	JACK HAWKINS
Richard de Beauchamp, *Earl of Warwick*	E. LYALL SWETE
Chaplain de Stogumber	LEWIS T. CASSON
Peter Cauchon, *Bishop of Beauvais*	EUGENE LEAHY
Warwick's Page	SIDNEY BROMLEY
The Inquisitor	O. B. CLARENCE
D'Estivet, *Canon of Bayeux*	RAYMOND MASSEY
De Courcelles, *Canon of Paris*	FRANCIS HOPE
Brother Martin Ladvenu	LAWRENCE ANDERSON
The Executioner	VICTOR LEWISOHN
An English Soldier	KENNETH KENT
A Gentleman	MATTHEW FORSYTH

Ladies of the Court : LILIAN MOUBREY   JULIET MANSEL
AGNES LAUCHLAN   ANNE HOWSE
ZILLAH CARTER

Courtiers, Monks, Soldiers, etc. :

ANTHONY CLARK   DESMOND DEANE   JACK EVERS
CASWELL GARTH   CHARLES MELLER   CECIL RAYNE
GUY VIVIAN   CHRIS WALKER

Jack Hawkins and Sidney Bromley are Pupils of Miss Italia Conti.

*Lawrence Anderson
as Brother Martin Ladvenu*

*Sybil Thorndike as Joan
Kenneth Kent as An English Soldier*

The Epilogue: Ernest Thesiger as Charles V11
Sybil Thorndike as Joan

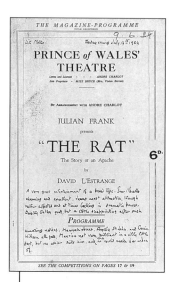

'With Mother.

A very good entertainment of a broad type - Ivor Novello charming and excellent. Isabel Jeans most attractive, though rather affected and at times lacking in dramatic power. Dorothy Batley good, but a little disappointing after such amazing notices. Hannah Jones, Dorothy St John and Cronin Wilson all good. Maurice [Braddell] not very brilliant in a silly little part, but one which suits h im, and which he could make far more of.'

Thinly concealed behind the nom-de-plume of David L'Estrange were Ivor Novello himself and the actress Constance Collier. Novello was, of course, well known as a song writer and composer, but this was his first play; the drama of Montmartre and the Apache life, together with Novello's matinée idol popularity, kept it going for 282 performances and a subsequent film.

Ivor Novello

Ivor Novello as The Rat

Ivor Novello as Pierre Boucheron - The Rat

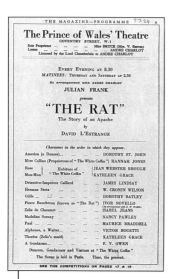

THE MAGAZINE—PROGRAMME 7·7·24 9

The Prince of Wales' Theatre
COVENTRY STREET, W.1

Sole Proprietor — — — Miss BRUCE (Mrs. V. Barron)
Lessee — — — — ANDRE CHARLOT
Licensed by the Lord Chamberlain to ANDRE CHARLOT

EVERY EVENING AT 8.30
MATINEES : THURSDAY AND SATURDAY AT 2.30

By arrangement with ANDRE CHARLOT

JULIAN FRANK
presents

"THE RAT"
The Story of an Apache
by
DAVID L'ESTRANGE

Characters in the order in which they appear.

America (a Dancer) ... — DOROTHY ST. JOHN
Mère Colline (Proprietress of "The White Coffin") HANNAH JONES
Rose } Habitués of {JEAN WEBSTER BROUGH
Mou-Mou } "The White Coffin" {KATHLEEN GRACE
Detective-Inspector Caillard ... — JAMES LINDSAY
Herman Stetz ... ... — W. CRONIN WILSON
Odile ... ... — DOROTHY BATLEY
Pierre Boucheron (known as "The Rat") IVOR NOVELLO
Zélie de Chaumet ... — ISABEL JEANS
Madeline Sornay ... — NANCY PAWLEY
Paul ... ... — MAURICE BRADDELL
Alphonse, a Waiter ... — VICTOR BOGETTI
Thérèse (Zélie's maid) ... — KATHLEEN GRACE
A Gendarme ... ... — F. V. OWEN

Dancers, Gendarmes and Visitors at "The White Coffin"
The Scene is laid in Paris.   Time, the present.

SEE THE COMPETITIONS ON PAGES 17 & 19

Poster for the film

Ivor Novello in his dressing room

Novello and Isabel Jeans

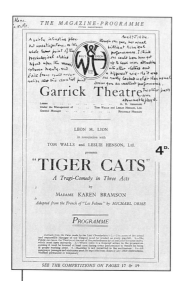

THE *MAGAZINE-PROGRAMME*

Garrick Theatre

Lessee .. .. A. E. ABRAHAMS
Under the Management of .. .. TOM WALLS and LESLIE HENSON, Ltd.
General Manager .. .. REGINALD DENHAM

LEON M. LION

in association with

TOM WALLS and LESLIE HENSON, Ltd.

presents

4ᴰ·

"TIGER CATS"

A Tragi-Comedy in Three Acts

by

MADAME KAREN BRAMSON

Adapted from the French of "Les Felines" by MICHAEL ORME

PROGRAMME

SEE THE COMPETITIONS ON PAGES 17 & 19

'Alone. In the Pit.

A fairly interesting play but unsatisfactory, as the whole point of the psychological studies depend upon the woman's extreme beauty - and Edith Evans could never realise this essential point, though she gave her usual brilliant technical performance. I think she could have been got up to look more attractive with other clothes and a different wig. As it was she really looked uglier than usual. Loraine gave an excellent performance. The other parts were abominably played.'

In spite of Gielgud's somewhat ungracious comments the public and the critics were more convinced by Edith Evans' ability to 'think beautiful', and the play ran for over 100 performances including a transfer to the Strand Theatre.

Arthur Wontner as Andre Chaumont
Edith Evans as Suzanne

Edith Evans as Suzanne

The Playhouse
Sole Lessee · FRANK CURZON.

"White Cargo"
BY
LEON GORDON.

PRICE · SIXPENCE

'With Gwen Ffrangçon-Davies.

Very good melodrama, admirably written and worked out, on an unpleasant theme. Hodges gave a performance as fine as anything I have ever seen on the stage - and Dyall was excellent.

Brian Aherne was very good, except for an occasional common note in his voice, sounding like Cockney - he should be very excellent after a few more jobs. Miss Sawyer did well the little she had to do - and everyone else was adequate, except Gordon Bailey who played an effective part badly.'

The 'unpleasant theme' referred to is the demoralisation which takes place when white men live in the hot, damp, exhausting climate of Africa and are exposed to the temptations offered by whisky and a dusky Delilah! The latter part was originally played by Mary Clare, later by Dorie Sawyer; the censor apparently objected to her scanty costume and she was obliged to cover up her bare midriff and cut down on the amount of visible thigh. With publicity like that, it was no wonder that the play ran for over 800 performances. Horace Hodges had a long career as a character actor - this was one of his finest efforts. Brian Aherne got a few more jobs and went on to a successful career in films.

Gielgud's theatre-going companion, Gwen Ffrangçon-Davies, had played Juliet to his Romeo at the Regent Theatre in May of this year, the beginning of a friendship which would endure for the rest of their long lives.

Horace Hodges was for a long time a valued member of my great-uncle Fred Terry's company, and was a superb Chauvelin in 'The Scarlet Pimpernel'. I think his last stage appearance was in 'A Hundred Years Old' at the Lyric Hammersmith. Check this. [In fact, his last stage appearance seems to have been in a revival of 'White Cargo' at the Cambridge Theatre in 1935 when Hodges was 70 years old.]

His sudden luck in 'White Cargo' was an example of a splendid actor being suddenly recognised by being given a fine opportunity. This has recently been far more usual with the huge audience provided by television, in which many hitherto unknown players have achieved stardom in their later years, such as Patrick Wymark, Joan Hickson and John Thaw.

J.G.,1993

Brian Aherne as Langford
Mary Clare as Tondeleyo

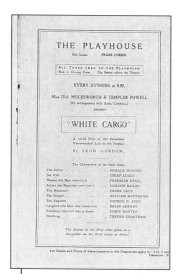

THE PLAYHOUSE

Sole Lessee · FRANK CURZON.

ALL TUBES LEAD TO THE PLAYHOUSE.
Book in Charing Cross. The Station adjoins the Theatre.

EVERY EVENING at 8.30,

Miss IDA MOLESWORTH & TEMPLER POWELL
(By arrangement with EARL CARROLL)
PRESENT

"WHITE CARGO"

A vivid Play of the Primitive
Unvarnished Life in the Tropics
By LEON GORDON.

The Characters as we meet them:

The Doctor	...	HORACE HODGES
Jim Fish	...	CHIEF LIALE
Weston (the Man who stays)	...	FRANKLIN DYALL
Ashley (the Man who goes home)	...	GORDON BAILEY
The Missionary	...	FRANK LACY
The Skipper	...	WILLIAM MATTHEWS
The Engineer	...	GEORGE D. AYRE
Langford (the Man who comes out)	...	BRIAN AHERNE
Tondeleyo (the Girl who is there)	...	DORIE SAWYER
Worthing	...	TREVEN GRANTHAM

The Action of the Play takes place in a
Bungalow on the West Coast of Africa.

For Details and Prices of Advertisements in this Programme apply to: THE WEST
Telephone: R

Brian Aherne as Langford

'Kiss me! Kiss me!'
Franklin Dyall as Weston
Mary Clare as Tondeleyo

Horace Hodges as Doctor

PART 1 'With Angus.

Very fine and magnificently acted by Gwen [Ffrangçon-Davies] and Edith Evans, the men adequate without being exceptionally good. Gwen as the old Eve was really amazing - I had no idea she could do anything so perfectly.'

PART V 'With Angus.

A good deal less interesting than Part I, in spite of brilliant performances by Hardwicke, Gwen and Edith Evans. Very long and the small parts very badly played. Wretched costumes. Miss Chatwin quite fine as Lilith.'

Shaw had little hope of his cycle of plays on Creative Evolution ever being a financial success; his reply to Barry Jackson's request for the play was: "Is your family provided for?" His Birmingham production of the full cycle had played at the Royal Court earlier in the year, and these special matinées of Parts I and V were given during the long run of 'The Farmer's Wife'.

Cedric Hardwick, who was knighted in 1934, had a long and distinguished career in this country and in the United States. He was particularly noted for his performances in Shaw's plays and was the first British actor to play King Magnus in 'The Apple Cart'.

Colin Keith-Johnston as Adam
Gwen Ffrangçon-Davis as Eve
Edith Evans as The Serpent

'Very brilliant play, with a fine third act. Witty, effective and original. Not awfully well acted, but Mollie Kern, Davenport and Millie Sim were excellent, and Lilian Braithwaite, in a magnificent part, has never done anything better. Coward himself lacked charm and personality and played the piano too loudly, though he acted sincerely and forcefully as far as he could. The play is certainly an amazing achievement for him, and the end of the 2nd act and all the third are really fine.'

Although 'The Young Idea' and 'I'll Leave it to You' had met with moderate success, it was 'The Vortex' which really established Coward as a playwright. The Hampstead production transferred to the West End, where it ran for over 200 performances.

Lilian Braithwaite, who was created D.B.E. in 1943 was highly regarded throughout her long career. An actress of great range, she was probably better known for her work in contemporary plays than the classics. Her daughter, Joyce Carey, followed in her mother's footsteps.

Gielgud was still working at the Oxford Playhouse in 1925, but when 'The Vortex' transferred to the Royalty Theatre he was asked to understudy Coward as Nicky Lancaster in the production, and appeared for him when Coward wanted to see the opening of his new revue, 'On with the Dance', in Manchester. The production later moved to the Little Theatre, and Gielgud played for three weeks when Noël Coward took a holiday before going to America with the play.

Nöel Coward as Nicky Lancaster
Lilian Braithwaite as Florence Lancaster

'With Angus and the family.

Good setting in the last act, otherwise not very good decor. Musical comedy production. Petrie, Gwen and Athene Seyler and Quartermaine all good. Evans, Jeayes, Bobbie Harris and Walter poor. Other comics good. Far too much ballet.'

Another Basil Dean spectacular with music by Mendelssohn, ballets by Michael Fokine, a large choir, 21 fairies and 5 gnomes!

I didn't like it at all. Edith Evans was so disappointed by her own performance as Helena that she decided to go to the Old Vic to learn how to play Shakespeare.

Gwen Ffrangçon-Davies was charming as Titania, but the Wood scene was hideously ugly with slopes and hillocks which forced the actors to rush about in every direction while ballet intruded disastrously.

J.G.,1993

The play scene

Gwen Ffrangçon-Davis as Titania
Wilfrid Walter as Bottom

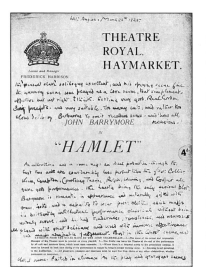

'With Angus.

The 'peasant slave' soliloquy excellent, and his opening scene fine. The nunnery scene was played as a love scene, tout simplement - effective but not right, I think. Setting very good. Real Gordon Craig precepts and very suitable. Too many cuts and rather too slow delivery. Barbarous to omit recorders scene - and "How all occasions".

An enthralling and in some ways an ideal production, though the last two acts are considerably less perfect that the first. Collier, Keen, Compton, Courtenay Thorpe, Relph, Waring, and Cooper all gave good performances - the Laertes being the only serious blot. Barrymore is romantic in appearance and naturally gifted with grace, looks, and a capacity to wear period clothes, which makes his brilliantly intellectual performance classical without being unduly severe, and he has tenderness, remoteness, and neurosis all placed with great delicacy and used with immense effectiveness and admirable judgement. Best in the Ghost scene and closet scene. Failed in climax in the play and graveyard scenes.'

The American actor John Barrymore's 'Hamlet', which he also directed, was probably the high point of his career and a performance which Gielgud admired greatly. Barrymore's production had set a record for the performance of the play on Broadway, a record broken eventually by Gielgud's own performance in 1937. The Craig-like settings were by Robert Edmund Jones.

John Barrymore as Hamlet

THEATRE ROYAL,
HAYMARKET.
Lessee and Manager - - FREDERICK HARRISON

Every Evening at 8 o'clock.
Matinées: Every Thursday and Saturday at 2 o'clock.

SHAKESPEARE'S

HAMLET

Claudius, *King of Denmark*	MALCOLM KEEN
Hamlet, *Son to the late, Nephew to the present King*	JOHN BARRYMORE
Polonius, *Lord Chamberlain*	HERBERT WARING
Horatio, *friend to Hamlet*	GEORGE RELPH
Laertes, *Son to Polonius*	NIGEL CLARKE
Rosencrantz	JEVAN BRANDON-THOMAS
Guildenstern *Courtiers*	MICHAEL HOGAN
Osric	FREDERICK COOPER
A Priest	HARDING STEERMAN
A Messenger	STANLEY ROBERTS
A Gentleman	HERBERT WHITMAN
Bernardo	ROY TRAVERS
Marcellus	JOHN MICHAEL
Francisco	A. G. POULTON
Player King	E. HARCOURT WILLIAMS
Player Queen	ARNOLD BOWEN
Player King	BURBEL LUNDBEC
Player Queen *In the Play*	BYAN SHAW
The Poisoner	VADIM URANEFF
First Grave Digger	BEN FIELD
Second Grave Digger	MICHAEL MARTIN-HARVEY
Fortinbras, *Prince of Norway*	SHAYLE GARDNER
Ghost of Hamlet's Father	COURTENAY THORPE
Gertrude, *Queen of Denmark, Mother to Hamlet*	CONSTANCE COLLIER
Ophelia	FAY COMPTON
Gentlewoman	PEGGY WEBSTER

Court Ladies—ALLISON LEGGATT, GRACE O'CONNOR, JOAN BYFORD, MAUD LESTOCQ, VERA ROGGETTI.
Courtiers—H. HUMBLESTONE WRIGHT, CLAUDE RASFORD, ERIC LESTER, RUSSELL SEDGWICK, RICHARD TURNER, FRANK EDGAR.

The Play produced by JOHN BARRYMORE.

Constance Collier as Gertrude
John Barrymore as Hamlet

John Barrymore as Hamlet

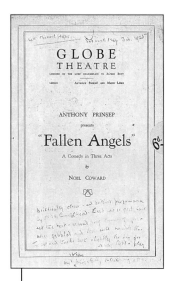

'With Michael Hogan.

Brilliantly clever - and brilliant performance by Miss Bankhead. Best not so good. Last act the best - second very amusing - first rather gabbled and less well rounded off. The set and theatre both slightly too big for so very light a play, but it was delightfully entertaining all the same.'

The play had been bought by the producer, Anthony Prinsep, as a vehicle for Margaret Bannerman. She had a nervous breakdown during rehearsals and was replaced by Tallulah Bankhead. The press notices were quite vituperative, according to Coward, but epithets such as 'vile', 'obscene' and 'degenerate' have always been very good for the box office, and the play ran for several months.

There were even protests in the theatre. 'The last performance at the Globe Theatre on Saturday night of Mr Noël Coward's much-discussed play 'Fallen Angels' was made the occasion of a protest by a Mrs Hornibrook, who had resigned her membership of the London Council for the Promotion of Public Morality in view of her fellow-members' dislike of public protests. At the end of the second act she stood up in a box and began to speak against the play, but her words were drowned by the orchestra, which began to play 'I Want to be Happy'. (Raymond Mander and Joe Mitchenson, 'Theatrical Companion to Coward').

Tallulah Bankhead as Julia Sterroll
Edna Best as Jane Banbury

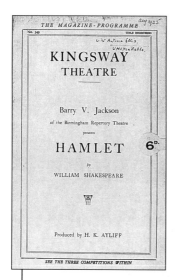

THE MAGAZINE-PROGRAMME *aug 1925*

No. 549   TITLE REGISTERED

with Antonia Ellis,
UNspeakable.

KINGSWAY
THEATRE

Barry V. Jackson
of the Birmingham Repertory Theatre
presents

HAMLET   6ᴰ·

by

WILLIAM SHAKESPEARE

Produced by H. K. AYLIFF

SEE THE THREE COMPETITIONS WITHIN

'With Antonia Ellis.

UNspeakable.'

The Victorian proposition of 'historically accurate' Shakespeare, begun mainly by Charles Kean and continued by Tree and Irving still held a firm grip on theatregoers' consciousness. This was the famous (or notorious) modern dress production for the Birmingham Repertory Theatre, directed by H.K. Ayliff. Sir Barry Jackson, the founder of Birmingham Rep. believed strongly that Shakespeare's plays did not depend on externals and a modern dress production of 'Cymbeline' had been done in Birmingham in 1923 and before this London production, Ayliff had done a modern dress version of 'Hamlet' in Vienna which had been enthusiastically received. London was therefore unprepared for the experiment, and although most of the serious critics recognised its validity, it created a considerable furore - The Men's Wear Organiser was of the opinion that 'Hamlet's evening kit was a sheer disgrace' - he wore a soft shirt and collar with a dinner jacket. There is no doubt about the young Gielgud's feelings, although these were apparently not strong enough to prevent him playing Rosencrantz in two special matinées of the same production at the Royal Court the following year!

Known as 'Hamlet in plusfours', I could not reconcile myself to this experiment, of which there have been so many like it since. Frank Vosper was a splendid Claudius but Colin Keith-Johnston could not touch Hamlet. Ophelia was charmingly played by Muriel Hewitt , who was to marry Sir Ralph Richardson.

The graveyard scene was the most effective, but not so impressive as the one in Tyrone Guthrie's later modern dress revival of the play when everyone carried umbrellas.

J.G.,1993

Colin Keith-Johnston as Hamlet

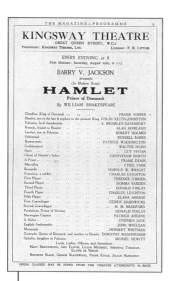

THE MAGAZINE—PROGRAMME   9

KINGSWAY THEATRE
GREAT QUEEN STREET, W.C.2
Proprietors : KINGSWAY THEATRE, LTD.   Licensee : F. R. LITTLER

EVERY EVENING AT 8
First Matinee: Saturday, August 29th, at 2.15

BARRY V. JACKSON
presents
(In Modern Dress)

HAMLET
Prince of Denmark
By WILLIAM SHAKESPEARE

Claudius, King of Denmark	FRANK VOSPER
Hamlet, son to the late & nephew to the present King	COLIN KEITH-JOHNSTON
Polonius, lord chamberlain	A. BROMLEY-DAVENPORT
Horatio, friend to Hamlet	ALAN HOWLAND
Laertes, son to Polonius	ROBERT HOLMES
Voltimand	RUSSELL BARRY
Rosencrantz	PATRICK WADDINGTON
Guildenstern	WALTER HUDD
Osric	GUY VIVIAN
Ghost of Hamlet's father	GROSVENOR NORTH
A Priest	FRANK DENIS
Marcellus	CYRIL VANE
Bernardo	HAROLD W. WRIGHT
Francisco, a soldier	CHARLES LEIGHTON
First Player	TERENCE O'BRIEN
Second Player	NORMA VARDEN
Third Player	DONALD FINLAY
Fourth Player	CHARLES LEIGHTON
Fifth Player	ELANA AHERNE
First Gravedigger	CEDRIC HARDWICKE
Second Gravedigger	H. M. BRADFORD
Fortinbras, Prince of Norway	DONALD FINLAY
Norwegian Captain	PATRICK AHERNE
A Sailor	STEPHEN JACK
English Ambassador	JOHN MACLEAN
Messenger	HERBERT WHITMAN
Gertrude, Queen of Denmark, and mother to Hamlet,	DOROTHY MASSINGHAM
Ophelia, daughter to Polonius	MURIEL HEWITT

Lords, Ladies, Officers, and Attendants :
MARY BRAITHWAITE, AMY ELSTOY, LILIAN MOISSREY, VERONICA TURLEIGH, ELAINE DE VRIAN
KENNETH BLACK, GEORGE BLACKWOOD, FRANK EDGAR, JILLIAN HAMILTON

OPERA GLASSES MAY BE HIRED FROM THE THEATRE ATTENDANTS 6d. EACH

A.Bromley-Davenport as Polonius

The graveyard scene

Frank Vosper (L) as Claudius
Colin Keith-Johnston (R) as Hamlet

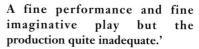

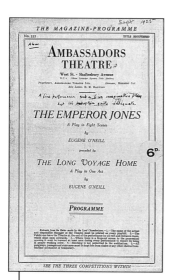

'Alone.

A fine performance and fine imaginative play but the production quite inadequate.'

The play and the part established Paul Robeson as the greatest black actor since Ira Aldridge, although he had already had considerable success in 'All God's Chillun Got Wings'. His first appearance in England was at the Opera House, Blackpool, in 1922, when he appeared with Mrs Patrick Campbell in a play called 'The Voodoo'.

Paul Robeson as Brutus Jones

THE MAGAZINE-PROGRAMME
No. 551   TITLE REGISTERED

BARNES
THEATRE

Licensee and Director . . . PHILIP RIDGEWAY

PHILIP RIDGEWAY

presents   **6**D.

"Tess of the D'Urbervilles"

A Tragedy

In Foreshow, Four Acts and an After-scene

by

THOMAS HARDY, O.M.

SEE THE THREE COMPETITIONS WITHIN

'With Mrs Ellis.

A bad play - Gwen [Ffrangçon-Davies] gave a superb and brilliant performance, though rather unsatisfying because she was so miscast - though her playing was faultless. Swinley was admirable. The Stonehenge scene alone satisfied me entirely. The rest marred by bad writing, lighting, and production, maddeningly silly comic relief and some pretty bad acting - notably by Trevor. Also the smallness of the stage was a continual handicap, and the essentials of the plot melodramatic and unconvincing for the purposes of the stage.

Whatever his reputation, there was general critical agreement that Hardy the dramatist was not in the same league as Hardy the novelist. Nonetheless, Hardy enthusiasts travelled to Barnes in their thousands and the play transferred to the Garrick Theatre for a short season later in the year.

The Russian director, Theodore Komisarjevsky, was to produce a season of Russian plays at the tiny Barnes Theatre the following year; he saw Gielgud playing Konstantin in a production of 'The Seagull' and invited him to play Tusenbach in his production of 'Three Sisters'. Komisarjevsky could be an inspired director and teacher, and his work had a powerful influence on the young Gielgud's acting. It was through his work in Barnes that the London critics began to take notice of the young actor.

Gwen Ffrangçon-Davies as Tess

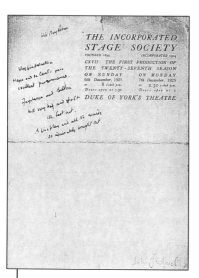

'**With Mary Robson.**

Very fine production. Hayes and de Casalis gave excellent performances. Farquharson and Beldon both very bad and spoilt the last act. A fine play and all the comedy so admirably brought out.'

This was the first London production of Chekhov's play. It is perhaps appropriate that the last programme in the collection is for a play in which Gielgud himself would appear with such distinction in his own adaptation and production forty years on.

By the end of 1925, John Gielgud was 21 years old and established as a young actor of talent and promise. Four years later he would return to the Old Vic at the invitation of Lilian Baylis and, by his performances in 'Romeo and Juliet', 'Richard II' and 'Hamlet', establish himself as the foremost young classical actor of his generation.

John Gielgud as Ivanov
Vivien Leigh as Anna Petrova (1965 production)
(Vivien Leigh played the part when the production crossed the Atlantic;
in London the part was played by Yvonne Mitchell.)

JOHN GIELGUD'S PLAYGOING

DATE	THEATRE	PLAY
No date 1917	Vaudeville	Cheep!
21 June 1917	Palace	Airs and Graces
1918		
No date 1918	Vaudeville Theatre	"Tabs"
No date 1918	Wigmore Hall	Pierrots and Orchestra of the 25th Division
No date 1918	Palace	Pamela
No date 1918	Palace	Hullo America
No date 1918	Wyndham's	Dear Brutus
June 1918	Globe	Nurse Benson
October 1918	Royal Court	Twelfth Night
1919		
January 1919	Lyric Hammersmith	Make Believe
12 April 1919	Lyric	Romeo and Juliet
Later 1919	Lyric	Romeo and Juliet
12 September 1919	Theatre Royal, Drury Lane	The Great Day
November 1919	Lyric	The Bird of Paradise
November 1919	Princes	The Mikado
December 1919	Princes	The Gondoliers
December 1919	Scala	Fifinella
1920		
No date 1920	Queen's	The Young Person in Pink
No date 1920	Theatre Royal, Haymarket	Mary Rose
No date 1920	London Hippodrome	Jigsaw
No date 1920	London Hippodrome	Aladdin
Late 1920	Theatre Royal, Haymarket	Mary Rose
January 1920	Aldwych	Sacred and Profane Love
January 1920	Royal Court	The Merchant of Venice
January 1920	St James's	Reparation
January 1920	St James's	Julius Caesar
5 January 1920	New Theatre	Mr Pim Passes By
February 1920	Aldwych	Pygmalion
May 1920	Lyric Hammersmith	As You Like It
May 1920	Lyric Hammersmith	Much Ado About Nothing
July 1920	Theatre Royal, Drury Lane	The Garden of Allah
July 1920	Strand	At the Villa Rose
9 September 1920	New	The Wandering Jew
November 1920	Everyman Hampstead	Romeo and Juliet
2 November 1920	Aldwych	Macbeth
December 1920	Lyric Hammersmith	The Beggar's Opera

1921

No date 1921	Palace	Romance (Film)
January 1921	Shaftesbury	The Great Lover
January 1921	St James's	Daniel
16 January 1921	Royalty	Milestones
25 January 1921	Playhouse	The Sign on the Door
February 1921	New Oxford	League of Notions
March 1921	Old Vic	Hamlet
April 1921	St Martin's	A Bill of Divorcement
6 April 1921	Theatre Royal, Haymarket	Quality Street
19 April 1921	Gaiety	Faust on Toast
21 April 1921	Royal Court	Othello
May 1921	Princes	Russian Ballet
4 June 1921	Princes	Russian Ballet
June 1921	Royalty	The Cinema Lady
25 June 1921	Princes	Russian Ballet
5 July 1921	Princes	Russian Ballet
9 July 1921	Princes	Russian Ballet
10 or 11 July 1921	Comedy	The Parish Watchmen
23 July 1921	Princes	Russian Ballet
26 July 1921	Lyric Hammersmith	The Beggar's Opera
28 July (mat.)1921	Princes	Russian Ballet
28 July (eve.) 1921	Princes	Russian Ballet
30 July 1921	Princes	Russian Ballet
30 August 1921	Lyric Hammersmith	The Beggar's Opera
12 September 1921	Ambassador's	If
15 September 1921	Lyric Hammersmith	The Beggar's Opera
17 September 1921	Old Vic	Much Ado About Nothing
3 October 1921	Old Vic	Richard II
8 October 1921	Queen's	The Hotel Mouse
15 October 1921	Theatre Royal, Haymarket	Quality Street
18 October 1921	Royal Court	Heartbreak House
20 October 1921	Aldwych	My Nieces
26 October 1921	Old Vic	Macbeth
2 November 1921	Alhambra	The Sleeping Princess
4 November 1921	Vaudeville	Now and Then
9 November 1921	Alhambra	The Sleeping Princess
14 November 1921	Old Vic	Wat Tyler
17 November 1921	Shaftesbury	Will Shakespeare
22 November 1921	Criterion	Ambrose Applejohn's Adventure
28 November 1921	Shaftesbury	Will Shakespeare
November 1921	London Coliseum	Variety
2 December 1921	Alhambra	The Sleeping Princess
7 December 1921	Queen's	Put and Take
9 December 1921	London Pavilion	Fun of the Fayre
14 December 1921	Wyndham's	Bulldog Drummond
20 December 1921	Globe	The Truth About Blayds

| 23 December 1921 | Shaftesbury | Will Shakespeare |
| 27 December 1921 | Princes | The Mikado |

1922

2 January 1922	London Hippodrome	Jack and the Beanstalk
9 January 1922	Old Vic	The Merchant of Venice
12 January 1922	Savoy	Hamlet
13 January 1922	Old Vic	The Merchant of Venice
14 January 1922	Princes	Iolanthe
21 January 1922	Shaftesbury	The Rattlesnake
27 January 1922	Comedy	The Faithful Heart
29 January 1922	The Hampstead Conservatoire	The Bennets
2 February 1922	Alhambra	The Sleeping Princess
4 February 1922	His Majesty's	Cairo
5 February 1922	The Palladium	All Star Matinée in aid of the Actors' Employment Fund
6 February 1922	Old Vic	Othello
12 February 1922	Royal Opera House, Covent Garden	Atlantide (Film)
16 February 1922	Princes	Ruddigore
24 February 1922	Old Vic	Twelfth Night
March 1922	St Martin's	Loyalties & Shall We Join The Ladies?
3 March 1922	Duke of York's	The Enchanted Cottage
6 March 1922	Old Vic	Peer Gynt

JG walked on in this production

7 March 1922	Queen's	David Garrick
9 March 1922	Royal Court	The Pigeon
11 March 1922	Kingsway	The Yellow Jacket
14 March 1922	St James's	The Bat
20 March 1922	Vaudeville	Pot Luck!
3 April 1922	Royal Opera House, Covent Garden	Theodora (Film)
Week of 3 April 1922	London Coliseum	Variety
7 April 1922	Ambassadors	The Curate's Egg
11 April 1922	Palace	The Co-Optimists
17 April 1922	Old Vic	Love Is the Best Doctor & Comedy of Errors

JG walked on in Comedy of Errors

24 April 1922	Old Vic	Shakespeare Birthday Festival
25 April 1922	Royal Court	Windows
27 April 1922	Old Vic	Hamlet
1 May 1922	Palace	The Trojan Women
3 May 1922	New Oxford	Mayfair & Montmartre

8 May 1922	New Oxford	Mayfair & Montmartre
11 May 1922	St Martin's	Loyalties & Shall We Join The Ladies?
22 May 1922	Theatre Royal, Drury Lane	Decameron Nights
29 May 1922	Globe	Eileen
30 May 1922	Daly's	Amphitryon
3 June 1922	Royal Opera House, Covent Garden	Madam Butterfly
3 June 1922	Playhouse	The Second Mrs Tanqueray
5 June 1922	Royal Opera House, Covent Garden	The Twilight of the Gods
8 June 1922	Royal Opera House, Covent Garden	Tristan and Isolde
14 June 1922	Royal Opera House, Covent Garden	The Valkyrie
15 June 1922	Everyman Hampstead	You Never Can Tell
16 June 1922	Royal Opera House, Covent Garden	Siegfried
17 June 1922	Royal Opera House, Covent Garden	Tannhauser
20 June 1922	New Oxford	Chuckles of 1922
20 June 1922	Everyman Hampstead	Troilus and Cressida
22 June 1922	Princes	L'Illusioniste & Le Misanthrope
26 June 1922	Princes	Jacqueline
29 June 1922	Theatre Royal, Haymarket	The Dover Road
1 July 1922	Lyric Hammersmith	The Beggar's Opera
4 July 1922	Princes	Le Grand Duc
8 July 1922	Globe	Belinda
Week of 17 July 1922	London Coliseum	Variety
29 July 1922	New	Rounding the Triangle & Jane Clegg
19 August 1922	London Hippodrome	Round in 50
28 August 1922	Vaudeville	Snap!
31 August 1922	Queen's	Bluebeard's Eighth Wife
2 September 1922	His Majesty's	East of Suez
11 September 1922	Winter Garden	Primrose
13 October 1922	Globe	The Laughing Lady
15 December 1922	Little	The Nine O'Clock Revue
19 December 1922	New Oxford	Battling Butler
30 December 1922	Kingsway	Polly
1923		
January 1923	Prince of Wales	The Co-Optimists
1 January 1923	Strand	Treasure Island
2 January 1923	Lyric	Lilac Time
2 January 1923	Old Vic	Henry IV Part 2

4 January 1923	Little	The Nine O'Clock Revue
January 1923	Little	The Nine O'Clock Revue
6 January 1923	Empire	Arlequin
6 January 1923	Everyman Hampstead	Twelfth Night
11 January 1923	New Oxford	Battling Butler
16 January 1923	Apollo	A Roof and Four Walls
	JG co-designer	
10 February 1923	Royal Opera House, Covent Garden	You'd Be Surprised
15 February 1923	Wyndham's	The Dancers
20 February 1923	New Oxford	Battling Butler
24 February 1923	Kingsway	Polly
1 March 1923	Little	The Nine O'Clock Revue
13 March 1923	St James's	If Winter Comes
17 March 1923	St Martin's	The Great Broxopp
21 March 1923	Apollo	A Roof and Four Walls
22 March 1923	Criterion	Advertising April
24 March 1923	Playhouse	Magda
27 March 1923	Lyceum	The Orphans
7 April 1923	Everyman Hampstead	The Doctor's Dilemma
7 April 1923	His Majesty's	The Gay Lord Ouex
11 April 1923	Lyric	Lilac Time
11 April 1923	Strand	Anna Christie
12 April 1923	Criterion	Advertising April
14 April 1923	Royalty	At Mrs Beam's
16 April 1923	Old Vic	Hamlet
20 April 1923	Empire	The Rainbow
24 April 1923	St Martin's	R.U.R.
30 April 1923	Shaftesbury	Merton of the Movies
2 May 1923	New Scala	The Marionette Players
11 June 1923	Palace	Irving Berlin's Music Box Revue
12 June 1923	Apollo	What Every Woman Knows
12 June 1923	New Oxford	Spettri (Ghosts)
13 June 1923	London Pavilion	Dover Street to Dixie
14 June 1923	New Scala	The Marionette Players
15 June 1923	Little	The Nine O'Clock Revue
16 June 1923	His Majesty's	Oliver Cromwell
26 June 1923	Theatre Royal, Drury Lane	Ned Kean of Old Drury
4 July 1923	Prince of Wales	So This Is London!
11 July 1923	Criterion	Send for Dr O'Grady
24 July 1923	Theatre Royal, Haymarket	Success
25 July 1923	Aldwych	Tons of Money
27 July 1923	Ambassadors	The Lilies of the Field
4 August 1923	Duke of York's	London Calling!
10 August 1923	St James's	The Outsider
28 August 1923	Criterion	The Young Person in Pink
31 August 1923	St Martin's	The Will & The Likes of Her

September 1923	Little	The Nine O'Clock Revue
8 September 1923	Garrick	Ambush
19 September 1923	Kingsway	The Dark Lady of the Sonnets & Magic
21 September 1923	Ambassadors	The Lilies of the Field
24 September 1923	New	Cymbeline
24 September 1923	Prince of Wales	So This Is London!
25 September 1923	New Oxford	Little Nellie Kelly
26 September 1923	His Majesty's	Hassan
27 September 1923	Theatre Royal, Drury Lane	Good Luck
29 September 1923	Globe	Our Betters
30 September 1923	Lyric Hammersmith	The Winter's Tale
1 October 1923	Everyman Hampstead	Ancient Lights
2 October 1923	Vaudeville	Yes!
5 October 1923	New Scala	The Russian Blue Bird Theatre
6 October 1923	Gaiety	Catherine
12 October 1923	Duke of York's	London Calling!
17 October 1923	New	The Lie
28 October 1923	RADA Theatre	Morgan Le Fay
31 October 1923	His Majesty's	Hassan
2 November 1923	Royal Adelphi	The Sakharoff Matinées
10 November 1923	Kingsway	Twelfth Night
14 November 1923	Queen's	The Little Minister
16 November 1923	Duke of York's	London Calling!
23 November 1923	Theatre Royal, Haymarket	The Importance of Being Earnest
1924		
February 1924	Playhouse	The Camel's Back
13 February 1924	Lyric Hammersmith	The Way of the World
22 March 1924	Comedy	Alice Sit By The Fire
26 March 1924	New	Saint Joan
27 March 1924	Duke of York's	London Calling!
27 March 1924	Ambassadors	The Way Things Happen
4 April 1924	Globe	RADA Students Performance
12 April 1924	Vaudeville	Puppets!
14 April 1924	Shaftesbury	A Perfect Fit
23 April 1924	St Martin's	The Forest
28 April 1924	Wyndham's	To Have the Honour
5 May 1924	Royal Opera House, Covent Garden	Das Rheingold
6 May 1924	Royal Opera House, Covent Garden	Die Walkure
7 May 1924	Royal Opera House, Covent Garden	Siegfried
12 May 1924	Comedy	This Marriage
14 May 1924	Globe	Our Betters
June 1924	Haymarket	The Great Adventure

22 June 1924	Royal Court	A Bag of Nuts & Punchinello
24 June 1924	Criterion	The Mask and the Face
29 June 1924	Regent	The Pleasure Garden
July 1924	Royal Court	The Farmer's Wife
6 July 1924	Royal Court	A Comedy of Good and Evil
12 July 1924	Lyric Hammersmith	Midsummer Madness
14 July 1924	Prince of Wales	The Rat
16 July 1924	Shaftesbury	Toni
17 July 1924	Vaudeville	Puppets!
18 July 1924	Everyman Hampstead	Getting Married
August 1924	Everyman Hampstead	The Man of Destiny & How He Lied to Her Husband
22 August 1924	St Martin's	In the Next Room
27 August 1924	Garrick	Tiger Cats
28 August 1924	Queen's	Pansy's Arabian Night
September 1924	Playhouse	White Cargo
10 September 1924	Royal Court	Back to Methuselah I
12 September 1924	Royal Court	Back to Methuselah V
19 September 1924	Ambassadors	Fata Morgana
2 October 1924	Queen's	The Claimant
13 October 1924	Royalty	Storm
30 October 1924	Everyman Hampstead	The Devil's Disciple
7 December 1924	New	The Man With a Load of Mischief

Week of
8 December 1924	London Coliseum	Russian Ballet
	Everyman Hampstead	The Vortex
12 December 1924	St Martin's	No Man's Land
15 December 1924	Ambassadors	The Grain of Mustard Seed

Week of
15 December 1924	London Coliseum	Russian Ballet
18 December 1924	Lyric Hammersmith	The Duenna
20 December 1924	Strand	La Chauve-Souris
24 December 1924	Haymarket	Old English
26 December 1924	Theatre Royal, Drury Lane	A Midsummer Night's Dream
29 December 1924	Regent	The Little Minister
29 December 1924	London Coliseum	Russian Ballet

1925
4 January 1925	New	The Fairway
7 January 1925	Ambassadors	The Pelican
5 February 1925	Grand, Putney	Jitta's Atonement
8 February 1925	Regent	King Henry IV Part II
8 March 1925	Princes	Tunnel Trench

24 March 1925	Ambassadors	Anyhouse
26 March 1925	Haymarket	Hamlet
30 March 1925	Prince of Wales	Charlot's Revue
31 March 1925	London Hippodrome	Better Days
5 April 1925	Aldwych	The Colonnade
16 April 1925	New Oxford	Kismet
20 April 1925	Kingsway	Caesar and Cleopatra
	Dress rehearsal	
22 April 1925	Theatre Royal, Haymarket	Ariadne or Business First
3 May 1925	Globe	Fallen Angels
16 May 1925	Lyric Hammersmith	The Rivals
19 May 1925	St Martin's	Spring Cleaning
26 May 1925	Ambassadors	The Torch Bearers
Week of 25 May l925	London Coliseum	Russian Ballet
7 or 8 June 1925	Wyndham's	Raleigh
20 June 1925	Queen's	Beggar on Horseback
27 June 1925	Palace	No No Nanette
28 June 1925	Scala	Rule a Wife and Have a Wife
2 July 1925	Adelphi	Iris
4 July 1925	Everyman Hampstead	The Wild Duck
5 July 1925	Royal Court	The Prisoners of War
6 July 1925	Regent	The Rehearsal
9 July 1925	Garrick	Rain
14 July 1925	St Martin's	The Show
16 July 1925	Savoy	Polly
August 1925	Kingsway	Hamlet
August 1925	Prince of Wales	Charlot's Revue
September 1925	Ambassadors	The Emperor Jones
10 September 1925	Barnes Theatre	Tess of the D'Urbervilles
25 September 1925	Prince of Wales	Charlot's Revue
7 October 1925	Prince of Wales	Charlot's Revue
16 October 1925	Royalty	The Playboy of the Western World
10 November 1925	Ambassadors	The Burgomaster of Stilemonde
6 December 1925	Duke of York's	Ivanoff

June 15. 52.

Dear Richard Mangan,

I find it rather hard to believe that the present generation will be much interested in these juvenile reminiscences of my boyhood, culled from old programmes given to Mander and Mitchenson by my Mother some thirty years ago or more. But if the publication of them should result in some money to support the wonderful collection they have put together, of course I have no objection. I have added some few notes when my memory has prompted me and I must confess to a certain nostalgia in looking through the book, which recalls so many happy memories of my naive but enthusiastic visits to the theatre of my youth.

Yours sincerely

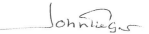
John Gielgud